"*Mr. & Mrs* is the best book on marriage I .... principles and practical insights are time-tested, creative, and biblical. I can't wait to recommend this gem to all of our marriage and family small groups and marriage mentoring team!"

Jeff Kennedy, D.Min.

Father, Son, and the Other One (Charisma House)

"A thoughtful, witty, and refreshingly candid book about marriage from a man who not only teaches, but lives the art of generosity. In a way no one else can, Bubna writes to the intimate, fundamental, humorous, and the practical with strokes of epic grace. Whether your marriage has weathered the storms or the ink is still fresh on the marriage certificate, *Mr. & Mrs.* is a great tool for learning to love one another well and commit to your marriage with your whole heart. A must read."

Tammy Strait

Pretty: Breaking Free From the Illusions of a Superficial Life and the blog grace uncommon

"As someone who has been a 'Mrs.' in a very imperfect marriage for 28 years, I was immediately drawn to the title of this book. Then the stories, insights, and wisdom found inside kept me hooked from cover to cover. In a culture headlined by divorce in the church, in Hollywood, in our neighborhoods, and in our families, *Mr. & Mrs.* delivers practical ideas and principles for making you want to stay together for the long haul. Couples starving for hope, longing for healing, and desperate for hands-on, real-life ideas to make their marriage meaningful and fun again will find Kurt's book a refreshing, down-to-earth read. *Mr. & Mrs.* will give you pause—and reason—to stay together.

Cornelia Becker Seigneur
WriterMom Tales
Founding Director, Faith & Culture Writers Conference

"*Mr. & Mrs.* is an honest look at marriage, crafted with humor and anecdotal truths. Pastor Kurt's approach is pleasantly conversational, and any married or potentially married couple will be encouraged by this handbook of inspiring insights."

Jan Cline
The Greatest of These is Love

"For 15 years I've used Kurt Bubna's material on relationships to train marriage mentors and counsel couples. Finally, he's brought it all together in one concise book that will help anyone who is serious about having a fulfilling marriage. His humor and insight are woven wonderfully into practical, timeless wisdom aimed at giving couples the skills they need to thrive. Any couple, regardless of their strengths or weaknesses, will benefit from this read."

Brian P. Ahlquist

Professional Counselor

"Kurt has an engaging style of communicating, and his practical, straightforward, encouraging message on covenant love and marriage will boost your marriage no matter its stage."

Matt Clark

Couples and Family Pastor, Life Center Church

Mr. & Mrs.

How to Thrive in a
Perfectly Imperfect Marriage

A Christian Marriage Advice Book

By Kurt W. Bubna
with Blake Atwood

Essential Life Press
vital resources for the christian life

Mr. & Mrs.: How to Thrive in a Perfectly Imperfect Marriage
(A Christian Marriage Advice Book)

Cover design by Theresa Farnsworth
(Shot by Tess: shotbytess.wordpress.com).

Published by Essential Life Press (EssentiaLifePress.org)
15303 E. Sprague Ave STE A.
Spokane Valley, WA 99037

All scripture quotations, unless otherwise indicated, are taken from the Holy Bible, New International Version®, NIV®. Copyright ©1973, 1978, 1984, 2011 by Biblica, Inc.™ Used by permission of Zondervan. All rights reserved worldwide. www.zondervan.com The "NIV" and "New International Version" are trademarks registered in the United States Patent and Trademark Office by Biblica, Inc.™

Scripture quotations are taken from the Holy Bible, New Living Translation, copyright ©1996, 2004, 2007, 2013 by Tyndale House Foundation. Used by permission of Tyndale House Publishers, Inc., Carol Stream, Illinois 60188. All rights reserved.

The stories in *Mr. & Mrs.* are true, but some names and identifying details have been altered to protect the privacy of those individuals.

ISBN-10:0692301070
ISBN-13:978-0692301074 (EssentiaLife Resources)

To Laura,

my amazing wife

and best friend

for nearly forty years.

Introduction

Introduction

Many years ago, the pastor who married my wife Laura and me told us: "Marriage is hard!" I was eighteen years old (yes, I was young), and I remember thinking, *"That might be true for you or others, buddy, but not for us. We've got this marriage-thing handled."*

That was my first marital mistake, and I made it even before my wedding vows. It only took me about a month of not-so-marital bliss to conclude that, marriage is indeed difficult.

What you hold in your hands is the product of many lessons learned over almost four decades of marriage. What you're about to read may be raw at times, certainly real, and sometimes even a bit radical. However, the principles you will find here are both biblical and practical. They are lessons learned in the trenches of a life together, precious truths about love, sex, communication, forgiveness, and much more.

You may not agree with everything I believe or write. You may find it challenging. But I pray you will be encouraged. Read each chapter with an open heart and I promise you will find Jesus and his grace and truth here.

I commend you for investing in your marriage. It takes guts to admit you might not know it all, and humility to acknowledge your weaknesses. But marriages develop through intentional and faithful dedication to the process of growth and change.

About five years into our marriage, I fell away from the Lord and "out of love" with my wife. Without a doubt, the most painful words she ever heard from me were, "I don't love you anymore. I want a divorce." My heart still aches over the angst I caused her that dark day long ago. Our marriage was a mess because I was a mess, but that's not the end of the story. Jesus never gave up on me and neither did my dear wife. Their love won me back.

It's what love does. It holds on, and it heals.

With that in mind, let's get started.

1

Take a Vow

IF TRAGEDY STRUCK your marriage, would it survive?

This isn't an unanswerable question.

In fact, I believe anyone can answer that question in the affirmative, but it requires a biblical understanding of the difference between covenantal and contractual relationships.

But first, a story to answer that question:

If I had to hazard a guess as to why Elizabeth fell for Robert, I'd go with physical fitness. When they wed, the dude was athletic, the kind of guy anyone would choose first in a game of flag football. One day, Robert was working beneath his pickup truck on his driveway. The jack somehow became dislodged, and two tons of metal crushed him, severing his spine.

Instantly paralyzed from his chest down, Robert's world likewise instantly changed.

He could no longer walk, so he couldn't work out or play the sports he loved.

He could no longer work as he used to, so he couldn't financially support his household.

He could no longer feel anything beneath his waist, so he couldn't have a sexual relationship with his wife, ending their ability to have children.

This is tragedy on an epic, Shakespearian, Job-like scale. This is an event with the power to derail even the most consistent and loving of marriages. This is a hard and serious way to begin a book about marriage, but there's a bright beacon of hope at the end of this seemingly dark tunnel.

Robert and Elizabeth are real, and they're people I'm proud to call friends.

Not only did they survive Robert's accident and everything they lost as a result of it, they *thrived*. They have one of the best marriages I've ever witnessed.

Why?

Because their love for each other isn't contractual; it's covenantal.

Contract and Covenant: What's the Difference?

Understanding and accepting the truth of the covenant relationship in marriage is one of the most important keys to enjoying a lasting marriage.

For most people in our society, marriage is a contract, a relationship based on perfect performances and fleeting feelings. To these same people, and to many Christians as well, the concept of a covenant relationship is a foreign idea. When people marry into a contract relationship, they view the marriage as simply an "agreement" between two people that can be broken at any time, for any reason, by either party. In their hearts and minds, this contract has little to do with God. Consequently, though most people in society deem divorce destructive and harmful, divorce is still a normal, acceptable recourse for a marriage gone south.

This is why it's paramount that we as Christians have a full understanding of the difference between covenant marriage (what God wants) and contract marriage (what we want).

1. A contract marriage is based on performance. A covenant marriage is based on my choice to remain faithful to my word and vows.

When a marriage is based on either spouse's performance, the relationship becomes plagued with if-then peril. In other words, when one marriage partner violates their part, the other person feels free to break off the marriage because their personal "commitment" was based upon their spouse's performance. For example, one spouse may demand a certain standard of living. If the other spouse can't provide for that need, the first spouse may threaten to leave.

Such a performance-based relationship creates a fragile atmosphere where love, acceptance, and permanence are all based on performance. Marriages crumble under such strain. Even more insidiously, we oftentimes fool ourselves into subconsciously helping to create these fragile environments. We may have performed our way into a marriage (think of what you did while dating your spouse that you seldom if ever do now), but it's utterly tiring to maintain a relationship based on performance.

But when a covenant replaces a contract, everything changes. Instead of focusing on my needs and my spouse's character, I focus on my character and my spouse's needs. Let me repeat that in a different way because it's been transformative in my marriage:

Covenant marriage focuses on my character and my spouse's needs, not my needs and my spouse's character.

Can you see how this small but significant shift in focus could strengthen your marriage? Of course, there's more to discuss, but this is an essential starting point.

When we say "I do" at the altar of a covenant relationship ceremony, we're vowing to our *own* commitment to love, cherish, and be faithful to our spouse. That statement is made with the firm belief and unyielding hope that our spouse will likewise fulfill their vow in the same way, but a covenantal commitment is *not* contingent upon their vow. By realizing this, such a relationship prevents "if-thenness" from infiltrating the marriage. Instead of one person pledging to remain faithful so long as the other person does too, each individual commits *to themselves* to remain faithful to their part in the marriage. As Ecclesiastes 5:5 reminds us, "It is better not to vow than to make a vow and not fulfill it."

When two people bind themselves to each other and to God through a covenant-based marriage, affirmation, acceptance, and confidence abound. No longer is each spouse accepted for *what they do or don't do*; rather, they're accepted for *who they are*. When we're accepted for who we are, we can freely share our deepest thoughts and feelings. We can speak the truth in love to each other without worrying about drastic relational repercussions.

Sounds a lot like the way God deals with us, doesn't it?

2. A contract marriage is rigid, unkind, impatient, and demanding. A covenant marriage gives the grace and freedom we each need to grow and develop.

My dear wife dances circles around me when it comes to grammar and writing, but she's not so good with numbers.

Some of our biggest fights have risen from the pages of our checkbook. I recall getting very upset with her one day regarding an error in our checking account, until I discovered that the error was my mistake. In that moment of humility, the Lord spoke to my heart. "Why is it so easy for you to forgive yourself, but not her?" After wincing internally from the pain of that cutting, insightful question, I apologized to Laura. Since then, I have an entirely different view of her "math mistakes" and choose to operate with much more grace toward her.

You'd think as an almost life-long pastor I'd know better, but I'm still human and a recovering idiot, and that's the major issue in any marriage.

One marriage equals one woman plus one man. Even if you're not good at math, that's two humans. And wherever two or more humans are gathered, disappointment and failure are sure to follow, especially in the pressure-cooker of marriage.

Pop culture may lead us to believe that relational failures can be fixed in thirty minutes or less, but we know better. Relationships are messy, but how we handle the mess reveals whether our relationships are rooted in covenant or pasted together in a contract.

A contract demands forgiveness for self and withholds forgiveness for the other.

A covenant freely forgives, especially when forgiving is hard.

A contract focuses on problems of the here and now.

A covenant looks to the future with eyes of faith and hope.

A contract cloaks itself in demands, cruelty, and impatience.

A covenant clothes itself in a patchwork quilt of grace, mercy, and patience.

A contract desires self-satisfaction above all.

A covenant seeks the good of the other, even in light of the other's sins.

A contract forgets what's already been forgiven them.

A covenant bears witness to Colossians 3:13: "Bear with each other and forgive whatever grievances you may have against one another. Forgive as the Lord forgave you."

3. A contract marriage is subject to dissolution based on a change of circumstances or the occurrence of problems. A covenant marriage provides protection, security, and peace regardless of circumstances or problems.

Had my friends Robert and Elizabeth not established their marriage on the basis of covenantal love, it's likely that their marriage wouldn't have endured such an incredibly difficult trial. Would you blame them if it hadn't? Hundreds of thousands of people in the U.S. divorce for lesser reasons. When a marriage is based on a contract, shifting circumstances and unforeseen problems rip the veil of security.

Contract marriages are often unprotected, insecure, and filled to overflowing with anxiety. After all, how could a person in such a relationship ever have sure footing? How could they know without a doubt where they stand in the relationship from their spouse's perspective? How could they know for sure if their marriage could endure the darkest of tragedies?

To be blunt, they can't. Consequently, anxiety takes hold and breeds insecure question after insecure question, eroding a person's trust in themselves, in their relationship, and in their spouse. Like a first-time sailor still seeking his sea legs, such a person will constantly scramble to secure their footing, fearful they might fall overboard at any moment.

Contract marriages allow either party to jump ship at the first onslaught of slightly distressing waves.

Covenant relationships, on the other hand, help marriages weather *any* "storms of change" that threaten to capsize their ship. Because each spouse has vowed to themselves and God to stick it out for the long journey before them, they can depend upon each other (and God) to help them through even the most difficult storms. They can face winds of adversity together regardless of what the world may throw at them.

As Ecclesiastes 4:12b reminds us, "A cord of three strands is not quickly broken."

4. A contract marriage leads to a fragile family future. A covenant marriage provides family security and a holy, healthy model for children and their future relationships.

You've likely heard divorced friends or family members trot out the line, "Well, we had to do it for the sake of the children." Though I'm not calling into question these parents' love for their children, I am casting doubt on their true reason for seeking a divorce. In other words, and pardon my bluntness, I think the "sake of the children" excuse is a crock of hooey. When I hear that phrase, my mind translates it to, "Because we won't change and learn to love each other unconditionally in covenant relationship, our kids are getting hurt, and neither of us wants that, so we need to divorce."

Of course, children who endure parents in constant, cruel, and ugly conflict will suffer. In such a dysfunctional and destructive home, such children will become insecure, depressed, disillusioned, rebellious, or all of the above. But the answer to preventing children from harm isn't to bail on the marriage and use the children as an "I'll take the high road" excuse. The answer is to get help so that both spouses can grow in their marriage and in their understanding of covenantal love. (Please go back and read the last line again. It's important.)

God didn't institute marriage for the sole reason of procreation. God meant for children to learn how to forgive, love, and accept others—warts and all—through what they see and experience within their homes. Establishing a marriage on the basis of a covenant will make a positive difference in the lives of your children *and* your children's children.

You likely know the stats as well as I do: children of divorce are much more likely to become divorced than children who've never suffered through their parents' separation. Children of divorce also tend to have a higher percentage of mental and physical illness and perform more poorly in school. When their home lives are so unsteady and out of their control, it's little wonder that they wrestle with such issues.

I would know. Well, my little brother and sister would know better.

When my parents divorced, I was already married and out of the house. Though I grieved my parents' divorce in my own way, my younger siblings had to deal with the present turmoil in their home. To be short, it messed both of them up big time. My sister didn't speak to my father for the next twenty years. By that time, she'd had three kids who had never met their grandfather, an issue that broke his heart and was tragic for all involved.

Don't tell me that kids just get over a divorce.

Tell me that you'll get over *yourself*.

Don't tell me that you're "doing it for the kids" when you know the stats regarding children of divorce.

Tell me that you're doing it for *you* without regard to your child's future.

Don't sugarcoat the bitterness of a divorce with the sweetness of a child.

Rather, be sweet to your child by ridding *yourself* of bitterness.

As the effects of a divorce can ripple throughout generations, so too can the hard work of an ongoing covenant marriage or two spouses seeking reconciliation. In pursuing each other at the sacrifice of self, parents at war can lay down their arms so that the crossfire doesn't strike innocent bystanders, forever wounding them and whatever generations might come from them. When children witness first-hand that level of forgiveness and acceptance, the ramifications are broad, deep, and eternal.

I want what Solomon wrote in Proverbs 17:6 to be true in my life: "Children's children are a crown to the aged, and parents are the pride of their children." To seek that crown, I pray this prayer for my children: "O God, let them have an even better marriage than I do. Let them learn their lessons more easily than I did. Let them experience even more of your goodness in a lifelong, covenant marriage. And God, help me model for them what it means to be a godly husband and parent."

I want to be proud of my kids and grandkids, but I also

want them to be proud of me.

Would that our eyes always be able to see their futures above our present circumstances.

To Seek a Covenant Relationship

If you're currently married, affirm (or reaffirm) your covenant relationship with your spouse. This can be as simple as telling him or her, "I love you for who you are and not what you do for me, and I'm committed to our relationship for the long haul no matter what storms may come." Remind yourself that the only strong, godly, and healthy foundation for a marriage is a covenant commitment.

If you're single and desire to be married someday, seek to learn what God expects of you in marriage. This book will open your eyes to the many issues than can arise within a marriage, but look for wisdom in the Bible first, and be sure to talk to God about what you're reading and learning.

If you've been divorced and are now remarried, set your heart on making your current marriage everything God desires it to be. Don't settle for anything less than covenantal love, even if (when!) times get tough. Remind yourself that covenantal love is the only way to survive and thrive in the midst of a world gone haywire.

Lastly, whether you're married, single, remarried, or

divorced, never forget that God makes covenant love possible. He is the ultimate example of unconditional, covenant love, and we would serve our spouses well by modeling our love for them after his love for us. Draw near to him and he will give you immeasurably more than all you ask.

Now ask yourself, "If tragedy struck your marriage, would it survive?"

2

Purposefully Unique

LET ME TELL you something you already know: from head to toe and body to soul, men and women are vastly different.

Let me tell you something else you already know: these *God-created* differences are the main source of marital conflict.

It's a conundrum, I know.

If he created us "male and female," why do our sharp edges always seem to cut those so near to us? Why would God create Adam and Eve for each other's pleasure only for marriage to become a frequent hotbed of conflict?

Essentially, why would he make us so different knowing that those differences could lead to so much pain?

I'm a pastor, so you can imagine how many couples in conflict I've listened to over the years. Jeff and Tonya are a real couple (with fake names) that represent so many Christian married couples that have come through my door with their heads hung low, defeated by each other.

They were college sweethearts who quickly married after graduation. They bought a nice house, landed good jobs, popped out two great kids, and bought a mini-van. All seemed well on the outside, but they were both changing. After six years of marriage, they'd grown to hate each other and wanted to file for divorce.

It's a cliché wrapped in a Christian version of a Lifetime movie, and it breaks my heart every time I see it play out in the lives of my church members.

I'm glad to report that they did seek counseling and God worked to bring them back together. But first they had to *unlearn* what they had accepted as truth about marriage and then begin understanding the very different relational needs of men and women.

The Cycle of Covenant Love

Now, not all marriages suffer under the weight of looming or ongoing conflict, but all committed marriages consistently cycle through the four recurring stages of covenant love: Romance > Trouble > Disillusionment > Joy.[1]

Most relationships start with the excitement of romance, all experience trials at some point, which typically leads to the valley of disillusionment or despair, but always ends in joy for those who stay the course. And joy leads to another season of romance!

However, if you think about it, each stage occurs *because* of the God-ordained differences between the sexes. And precisely half of the cycle is wonderful and intoxicating and half could be filled with bitter tears.

On this side of paradise, we're lucky for such an even split.

What I'm getting at is that men and women are different—and that's completely OK! When God created the sexes, he knew what he was doing. Knowing and appreciating our differences is crucial to having healthy relationships with the opposite sex. Recognizing that our differences will cause us to occasionally face trouble and disillusionment can help us persevere through those times and find joy and romance again.

Although this chapter will speak directly to women and then directly to men, I implore you to read the entire chapter. When I speak to your gender about the opposite gender, carefully consider how your differences may be causing more conflict than necessary in your marriage.

One of the most challenging yet fascinating aspects of covenant marriage is how God uses someone often so different from us to show us who we really are. Yet we're prone to shrink back from this reality because it likely means we need to change in some way, or admit fault, or learn to be less self-serving. Too often, we refrain from asking ourselves the hard questions about our relationships because we fear the answers might have far too much to do with ourselves.

Even if you have yet to marry, reading this chapter will help you understand the opposite gender's needs and desires, which can enhance *all* of your relationships with the opposite sex.

For the Women: What Men Want

I owe a debt of spiritual and marital gratitude to Willard F. Harley Jr. for his excellent book, *His Needs, Her Needs*. The following sections are adapted from that recommended resource for all covenant marriages.

Men are simple creatures. We may talk a good game, but all of our words hide four basic needs we seek from the fairer sex:

1. Unconditional love
2. Sexual fulfillment
3. A recreational playmate
4. Admiration

It's that simple, and no further words need be said about it. Now let's discuss what women need.

I'm kidding. While men's needs can be boiled down to a few basics, the underlying reasons for these needs are anything but simple.

Why Men Need Unconditional Love

As I said in Chapter 1, we all long to be loved unconditionally. This desperate though sometimes quiet yearning of our hearts exists because God placed it there. A covenant marriage ought to be a reflection of the kind of love God lavishes upon us, so both parties in a covenantal marriage ought to desire to receive and give unconditional love. Such love transformed the world, and it still has the power to transform relationships.

Ladies, if you don't believe me, make a pact with yourself to love your husband for a month without regard to his paycheck, his waistline, his temper, or any other measurable statistic. Love him for *who* he is and not *what* he's done for you—the same way Christ loves you.

Be warned though: showing unconditional love is hard and sometimes painful, but sacrifice often is. Yet be encouraged too. God will see your heart reflecting his kind of love and will help bring about the transformation in your marriage you long to experience.

Why Men Need Sexual Fulfillment

While not a man's top priority (whether they're aware of it or not), men need to feel sexually fulfilled within their marriage. Sex has become such a confusing, culturally degraded act that many new marriages begin to buckle when either spouse's sexpectations aren't met.

Yes, I said sexpectations, and if you're married, you know exactly what I mean. While this book contains an entire chapter on sex within covenant marriages, there are four important points to consider now in regard to men's need for sex:

1. God intends a man's sexual needs to only be fulfilled through marriage.

That means there's only one person who's ultimately responsible for meeting one of a man's major needs: you. Ladies, please understand and embrace this fact: God put you in his life as the only woman in the world your husband can engage with sexually without compromising his integrity or purity. So please see sex as a gift to your husband, not an obligation.

2. A man and a woman in a covenant relationship can have drastically different expectations for their sex life, often leading to disappointment, disinterest, or confusion.

Because men oftentimes lack communication skills, they may be a large part of their own problem. The only way a wife can ever know what her husband truly desires and expects is for her husband to *communicate* his desires and expectations.

3. Fulfilling a man's sexual needs is both important and biblical.

In 1 Corinthians 7:3-5, Paul writes, "The husband should fulfill his marital duty to his wife, and likewise the wife to her husband. The wife's body does not belong to her alone but also to her husband. In the same way, the husband's body does not belong to him alone but also to his wife. Do not deprive each other except by mutual consent and for a time, so that you may devote yourselves to prayer. Then come together again so that Satan will not tempt you because of your lack of self-control." God designed marriage as the place where a man and woman's sexual needs are met so that no one is unduly tempted.

4. Honest communication by both parties leads to the opportunity for mutual sexual satisfaction.

Chapter 3 will cover communication and how men and women can better learn to translate each other's words. What's amazing about honest communication, especially in regard to intimate matters, is that it often breeds more honest communication. This can hold especially true when a normally reticent husband finds confidence (and trusts God) to speak his mind in love to his wife. The following chapter will cover communication and how men and women can better learn to translate each other's words.

Why Men Need a Recreational Playmate

While this need could be misconstrued as just another way to say that men need sex, I mean something rather opposite. Men desire that the objects of their affection take interest in their hobbies or recreational activities. In essence, they want a friend with whom they can experience life.

Often, a woman will show interest in her man's activities when they're dating, but once they've wed, the woman will stop attending games or spending time with her man while he does "his thing." (Note: men are also guilty of the same behavior.) If such a couple doesn't become intentional about planning time to recreate together, a man may feel like something's missing from his life that he can't quite place.

To help in this area, brainstorm recreational activities with your husband that hold mutual appeal. Sure, there will be some activities that he suggests that only hold mild interest for you, but there will likewise be activities you suggest that hold mild interest for him. The key is to learn how to compromise for the betterment of the marriage. It's more about focusing on spending time together rather than focusing on what you're doing during that time.

Why Men Need Admiration

Some days I wonder if Jesus didn't talk about little children the way he did because he knows what little children we so often are on the inside.

Men are champion facade-builders, but when they're vulnerable they'll admit to the same self-doubt that plagues most people at their most insecure times. Men need support from those nearest them, and there is nothing stronger than the kind, honest praise of a wife. Such *spoken* admiration helps men believe in themselves despite their own swirling doubts.

Proverbs 27:15 paints a picture of a wife who fails to be supportive: "A contentious wife is like a constant dripping on a rainy day." Constant harping and negative criticism can damage a man's mental health and erode trust in his marriage. On the other hand, positive support can bring out his true potential.

So how can a wife express her admiration? Mentally identify your husband's positive characteristics, and then *verbally* tell him what they are and why you admire those specific qualities in him. Maybe he's an attentive father, or he's quick to forgive, or he's patient. Whatever it is, be sure to actually express your encouraging thoughts to him in some way on a regular basis. His confidence won't benefit if you only feel proud of him but never actually communicate it. For major bonus points, articulate those thoughts when you're together and when appropriate in a room full of friends or family.

Treating men as they wish to be treated encourages the character and behavior you desire from them.

In all things, remember that God desires the best for your marriage and has placed you with your husband for a reason. Believe that God is working on the character of the man in your life as you also work to meet his legitimate needs. By giving unconditional love, showing sexual interest, seeking shared recreational opportunities, and speaking your admiration, your marriage can't help but to grow closer, deeper, and better than ever before.

For the Men: What Women Want

Since women often seem more complicated than men, here are five basic needs they need met from the men in their lives:

1. Unconditional love
2. Authentic affection
3. Genuine honor
4. Stability
5. A spiritual partner

Why Women Need Unconditional Love

As we've covered, all of us have a deep and innate desire for unconditional love. We don't want a relationship complicated by performance clauses or a marriage that can't withstand changing circumstances. Women want to know and feel needed and loved, not for what they offer, but for who they are.

For the man who struggles with loving his wife unconditionally—regardless of her weight, income, interest in sex, or any other measurable characteristic—commit yourself for a month to loving her as Christ loves you. With God's blessing, your change can't help but to bring about positive changes in your marriage as well.

Why Women Need Authentic Affection

If I had to hazard a guess as to the common origin of so much sexually related strife in marriages, I'd bet my money on this need that so few men truly understand. Women desire affection, or non-sexual touch, but such touching often revs a man's engines long before a woman has even thought about picking up her keys. In other words, men are prone to misconstruing affection as foreplay. The kind of affection I'm talking about involves gentle touch (not genital touch, mind you) and caressing without sexual overtones of any kind. Such "hugs without horniness" can be difficult for men, but it's absolutely essential to meeting a woman's need for affection that such touching takes place minus the expectation of imminent sex.

In fact, a man fools himself into thinking he's serving his wife's need for affection when he chooses to manipulate that affection into meeting his own need for sex. While such affectionate attention does and can lead to sex, a husband's intentions should always work to serve his wife's needs first without any hidden (or not-so-hidden) agendas.

In fact, constantly shifting affection into sex may lessen a woman's desire for sex because her *deeper* desire for affection was never met in the first place! According to research on this topic, 80 percent of a woman's physical need is non-sexual. Additionally, the average woman needs eight to ten experiences of meaningful touch every day. When wives receive affectionate, non-sexual touches from their husbands, they're far more likely to be sexually responsive to their husband's needs.

It's a God-created give-and-take of each person meeting the other's needs, but when either side doesn't understand what the other's needs actually are, conflict is sure to erupt.

So, men: be intentional and constant with your affection, but not self-serving.

And remember: you're a microwave, but she's a slow cooker.

Why Women Need Genuine Honor

While women appreciate admiration from their husbands, to be treated with honor often means more. To honor your wife is to esteem, treasure, value, care for, and appreciate her, both for what she does and who she is.

Consider how you "honor" a prized material possession. For me, that's my guitar. I spend time with it. I clean it. I make sure it has new strings right before they're necessary. And I don't let anyone else play it. Now, I'm not saying that your wife should be treated like a material possession, but I am asking you to consider if you honor your wife as well or better than you might honor some other, lesser things in your life. How can you tell if you're honoring your wife?

When you speak to her, what's your general tone?

When you speak about her to others, what words do you use?

When you do something for her, what's your attitude while doing it?

When she's speaking to you, what's your level of attention?

We honor our wives with our tone, our words, our attitudes, and our attention.

Women in covenant relationships want to feel like they're the only one that matters to their husbands, and men can accomplish this by choosing to honor their wives on a daily basis. This means intentional listening as well as being open and honest about your own life. Women feel honored when men care deeply enough about them and the marriage itself to be vulnerable. Trust is a bedrock of the best marriages, and seeking to honor your wife through quality time and quality discussions is one of the best ways to establish such a foundation.

Why Women Need Stability

Many women desire that their husbands provide enough financial support for them and their family so that they can live comfortably. When children come into the picture, some women may also desire to stay home without feeling the pressure to work in order to sustain a certain standard of living. Yet this is only one aspect of stability that a woman may desire. She also wants her man to be a committed husband and father, someone who won't flee at the slightest threat or even the biggest obstacle.

If your wife may feel unstable or unsure about your future together, I encourage you to write a commitment note or letter. List the ways that you will work to provide for her physical, emotional, and spiritual needs. You don't have to use many words, and you don't have to make promises you can't keep, but be honest in your assessment of your current standing and your hopes for your marriage's future.

Again, clear and honest communication pays off during

conversations like these even though it may be challenging for both parties. Rely on God to help you seek stability if your marriage may be swaying in a rocking boat right now. When you show vulnerability by bringing your wife into your fears, then placing those fears in God's hands, you're serving her need for both honor and to have a spiritual partner. Plus, by taking proactive measures regarding her need for stability, you're showing your dedication to her and to the marriage.

Why Women Need a Spiritual Partner

We all need a spiritual partner, but Paul gave men a unique directive in his letter to the Ephesians: "Husbands, love your wives, just as Christ loved the church and gave himself up for her to make her holy." This sentence seems so simple, yet Paul later describes this passage as "a profound mystery," and it certainly is.

What does it truly mean for a man to love his wife as Christ loves the church? Let's consider the latter half of the question first.

How does Christ love the church?

- Consistently
- Personally
- Eternally
- Unconditionally

- Sacrificially
- Selflessly

These are all-encompassing terms, seemingly too grand for any one person to enact on their own. We're talking about God's abilities after all, which are timeless and omnipotent and omnipresent.

How can a fallen man reflect a perfect God?

"As Christ . . ."

Meaning we do so *in* him, *by* him, and *for* him.

Paul says that in Christ we're a new creation, and that the old has gone and the new has come. He's our conduit to a power much greater than our own. He's our go-between, our mediator, our High Priest. He's the only one who knows humanity inside out and divinity outside in.

He's our constant spiritual partner, the one we need in order to learn how to best love each other.

Men, that's what we're supposed to be to our wives, a living embodiment of Christ's love for us, their constant spiritual partner spurring them on to love and good deeds. Though we may often feel ill-equipped or bound by past sin to effectively lead our families in the way of Christ, we are implored to do so, and our marriages will suffer unless we carry that mantle.

It's a mystery indeed, but one we should never stop exploring.

What We All Need

Though every need mentioned in this chapter is a legitimate need, one need supersedes them all, and especially for two imperfect humans. Despite our incredible differences, men and women in covenant relationships need Jesus first and foremost. With him, working on meeting these needs may still be challenging, but you can rest assured that God will help your relationship thrive when you seek his will for your marriage.

Never forget: God is with you and you are not alone.

Now, let's talk about talking.

[1] The four recurring stages of covenant love are covered at length in "What Those Romance Novels Don't Tell You" from Chapter 12 of my first book, *Epic Grace*.

3

Say What?

DID YOU NOTICE how I didn't talk much about communication in the previous chapter?

The ways men and women communicate are yet another vast difference between the sexes, but it's such an integral part of a covenant relationship that we need to spend an entire chapter discussing it.

Whether you're a man or a woman, and regardless of whether you're single, dating, married, or divorced, you know this to be true.

You've spoken with an opposite-gender co-worker and can never seem to get your point across.

You've spoken with your opposite-gender parent and have felt like you're standing in front of a brick wall.

You've spoken with a platonic friend about a troubling issue, and you've squinted your eyes at their answer because it just doesn't make sense to you.

Though we are, for the most part, able to communicate fairly well across the great gender divide, we've all experienced notable moments of communication breakdown because of our innate male-female differences. Our everyday relationships typically don't suffer greatly because of these communication problems, but our *every day* marriages tend to bow under the constant pressure to know and be known by our spouse. (If you're unsure about the health of your marriage communication skills, take the quick, twelve-question communication inventory in the appendix.)

When our own husband or wife does not understand us in our own household, it can be maddening.

Like a slow-moving, unseen crack in a house's foundation, an inability to communicate well with your spouse will eventually cause your home to implode.

The Tim Taylor School of Communication

If you're a millennial, you may only know Tim Allen as the voice of Buzz Lightyear. But before leaping to infinity and beyond, Tim played Tim Taylor on the TV show Home Improvement. Allen based Taylor, a home repair show host, on himself and played off of stereotypical male behavior. Whenever confronted with a troubling issue, Tim would respond with a catchphrase-worthy grunt.

What's funny, and women the world over know this to be true, is that his grunt can be found in most men's vocabularies.

In fact, I have a friend whose primary love language is grunting. As an only child in an environment that he describes as one step away from "Hermitville," it could be argued that he came by it honestly. If I had to assess his communication skills from one to ten, he'd be minus three.

Can you imagine what his lack of communication skills did to his marriage?

Ponder what it must have been like for his wife to ask a question, then for his every reply to be some variant of "Urgh."

If you're a woman reading this book, you probably don't need to think about that illustration for long. You likely have your own stories to tell.

For the men, take my friend's story as a cautionary tale. His wife eventually had an affair. And while there are dozens of reasons for unfaithfulness (which we'll discuss in Chapter 6), a severe lack of communication can be the first unintentional nudge that ultimately pushes a spouse out of the home.

If you're a graduate of the Tim Taylor school of communication, don't be discouraged. I'm a pastor, so I get paid to communicate in many different ways . . . and I still wrestle with learning how to best converse with my wife. However, I try to show my wife I love her by always seeking to be a better communicator *with her.*

Though I'm challenging the men (because I fall into that category), women must likewise identify their own verbal shortcomings and learn how to better relate to their husbands.

The best kind of communication looks like a graceful give-and-take, an intentional dance that gives life to both partners.

But to make that dance happen, each person has to know their steps.

He Said, She Said

We intuitively understand that men and women communicate in different ways, but how do the sexes specifically differ?

Before diving into that question, we need a broad understanding of "communication." Talking is one aspect of communication, but it is by no means the only defining characteristic. (I think this is where most guys get into trouble by the way.) Communication encompasses what you say, but also the tone you say it in, the feelings you convey, the body language you show, as well as how you listen and work to understand the other person.

Like I said, good communication is a give-and-take experience. It exists *between* two people, not from one person to someone else.

Now, on to our major differences.

According to author Gary Smalley, most women primarily relate to their husbands through a "language of the heart" while most men tend to communicate to their wives through a "language of the mind." This isn't always true, but it is the norm for about 80 percent of households in the U.S.

In other words, women share their thoughts, feelings, goals, and dreams. They can also relate to others on multiple levels and in many directions at the same time. Men are typically logical, factual, detail-oriented, singularly focused, and reticent to share their deeper feelings or aspirations. They also usually relate to others on one level at a time and are adept at compartmentalizing their thoughts.

While our communication differences go much deeper, these are the broad issues that tend to wreak havoc on marriages. Though you likely have a sense of why this is so, you'll see proof of it in the next section.

The Five Levels of Communication

In *Why Am I Afraid to Tell You Who I Am?*, John Powell lists our five common levels of communication. Another way to think about these levels is to consider them five degrees of a person's willingness to disclose their thoughts and emotions:

1. Cliché communication occurs when we use everyday words and is most commonly heard at jobs or on elevators. For example, "How's the weather?"

2. Fact-reporting happens when we simply relate a story without embellishment or personal details. It's surface-level talk that requires nothing of the speaker and nothing of the listener.

3. Idea and opinion-sharing occurs when we share what we think about something. This is where a speaker begins to incur possible risk by sharing an opinion.

4. Feelings and emotion-sharing happens when we start to get real with ourselves and others and share what we feel about a situation. This is "gut-level" talk that reveals our hearts.

5. Peak communication occurs when a heart-to-heart connection takes place. Such communication requires honesty, openness, and fearlessness in the face of sharing your thoughts, feelings, and emotions. It also demands that a deep degree of trust, commitment, and friendship exists between the two parties. Peak communication happens when both people are transparent and willfully choose to understand and empathize with each other even when it's hard to do so.

Though life's circumstances can alter our levels of communication with our loved ones—just think of what you'd say to a parent on their deathbed—most of us tend to vacillate between only a few rungs on this communication ladder.

For instance, if I had to hazard a guess, most guys climb up and down between fact-reporting and opinion-sharing, and every once in awhile they'll reach the emotion-sharing rung just long enough to appease their wife. On the other hand, women may tend to alternate between fact-reporting, opinion-sharing, *and* emotion-sharing, likely staying toward the top of that ladder.

This is where we can easily visualize why our communication differences can cause harm. If you envision a husband and wife actually on this ladder of communication (for the sake of argument, let's say the rungs are spaced every twenty feet), they're seldom if ever on the same rung. One has to shout to the other even to be heard. Plus, while both of them may desire to achieve peak communication, they both have lots of work to do to get on the same level.

So what hinders our growth and progress?

Obstacles to Effective Communication

Before looking at the specific obstacles that tend to block our efforts at better communication, let's consider for a moment where our communications training might have originated. Knowing from where—or from whom—we receive our bad habits can help us work against those natural and unhealthy tendencies in our relationships.

A vast majority of our learned communication skills stem from our family. Were your parents "yellers" and raised their voice at you on a constant basis, or were they "silencers" and employed the silent treatment when you got in trouble? We're all significantly influenced by the family model we experienced. Pause here for a moment and consider the ways the family you grew up in communicated, then compare and contrast that with how *you* communicate today.

As for a more subtle point of origin, though we may be out of high school, we're still not immune to peer pressure. Whether we're totally aware of it or not, we pick up communication habits from those we're often near to, especially at places of employment and other areas of our lives where we're in persistent contact with other people. This can be especially damning to marriages when others' cynical view of marriage starts to erode our own perspective.

Lastly, mass media offers tantalizing, though oftentimes

hollow, models for effective communication. Film and TV make it seem as if the perfect words said at the perfect time in the perfect place will lead to the perfect ending. On the other hand, the rampant sarcasm displayed in many situation comedies pummels marriage in the real world. Either way, we believe such lies at our peril.

Again, pause here and consider how your family, friends, co-workers, and popular culture have influenced the way you communicate. Think about whether such habits benefit or harm your marriage.

Now let's look at seven common communication obstacles we all tend to stumble over at one point or another:

1. A preoccupation elsewhere

We know what this means because we're all guilty of it, and we've all been its victim. We see preoccupation in wandering eyes when a serious talk begins, in the thousand-yard stare when conflict arises, and in the not-so-subtle glance at a watch when someone asks, "Can we talk?"

Those whose minds drift elsewhere easily have likely not been intentional about setting apart distraction-free time to privately and honestly speak with their spouses. For some this means turning off the TV. For others it means setting down an iDevice. And for parents, it probably means waiting until you've put the kids to bed.

When a person's mind becomes so preoccupied with "elsewhere" thoughts, it's often not long until that person wants to *be* elsewhere. By learning how to focus when communicating with your spouse, as well as setting time apart to purposefully relate to each other, you will strengthen your marriage.

2. A tendency to play verbal ping-pong.

This happens when one person speaks and then impatiently waits for the other person's reply only so they can speak again. It's a me-centered type of communication that promotes self at the expense of others. It's only one-half of the give-and-take that's essential to healthy communication. A verbal ping-pong player is a loser of a listener, and a terrible listener is very likely unable to empathize well with others. Where there's a lack of empathy, relational conflict is sure to abound.

I'll say it again: communication isn't a game; it's a dance.

3. Unresolved issues.

This is a catch-all problem from which we all might suffer. Sometimes anger at a boss gets displaced onto a spouse. Sometimes frustration with a neighbor or a friend is taken out on your spouse. Let me be clear: using your spouse as a surrogate punching bag is not a good idea.

Another common issue needing resolution is unforgiveness. Bitterness is a weed that takes root in the heart. While the bitter person may think their rage is only directed at the object of their scorn, bitterness is sin and subsequently stretches its tendrils around anything else in its near vicinity. Living with a bitter spouse, even if that spouse isn't bitter at their mate, can be an intense relationship challenge.

These "invisible barriers" can bring slow ruin upon a relationship because neither party may be fully aware of what's really happening.

4. An unwillingness to relate as one adult to another.

It's tough to have an adult conversation with a thirty-year-old man-child or a twenty-four-year-old princess. Unfortunately, some people refuse to grow up. When one person acts like a child in a relationship, it can be very hard for the other to not always "parent" their spouse. Wives sometimes make jokes about their husbands being "like another kid," but there's unfortunate truth to many of those claims. Men sometimes treat their wives in a condescending manner, speaking to them in overly simplistic ways, or they have no idea how to relate to a self-absorbed and immature diva.

In an adult relationship, only adult conversation is healthy. Both parties must converse responsibly and without tit-for-tat childishness.

5. Language barriers.

In addition to their grunts, men have a certain "man-ese" language. Likewise, women speak "woman-ese." We might use the same words, but we often mean something completely different.

For example, when a man says, "I'm hungry. Let's get something to eat," he means *I don't care what or where I eat, I just want food, now!* However, when a woman says the same thing, she probably means, *I'd like to talk about our options and consider a variety of possibilities (as long as they have a nice atmosphere and a healthy green salad available).* You can imagine the ensuing conflict when he pulls into Taco Bell.

Likewise, when a woman says, "I need to do some shopping," the typical male thinks she has a specific list and a single store in mind, not wandering through the mall window-shopping for hours. For him, shopping is more like hunting: *Me find. Me kill. Me take home*; for her, it's akin to retail scrapbooking. (By the way, we have no idea what scrapbooking really is either.)

Both sexes ought to work on better understanding what the other sex actually means when they use certain words and even common phrases.

6. Poor self-image.

Those with poor self-images tend to downplay their ideas,

thoughts, and emotions. Consequently, they may seldom share what they really think or feel about a given situation. They may even verbally degrade themselves. A spouse of someone with a poor self-image likely won't bring up delicate or challenging topics for fear of hurting their spouse or getting hurt in some way. This prevents honest communication from having even a remote possibility of occurring. To make matters worse, someone with a poor self-image may feel like a victim in life, blaming their woes on everyone around them, and consequently not taking responsibility for their own actions and relationships.

7. A poor prayer life.

If you can talk to God about something, you'll have a better chance at talking to your spouse about the same issue with candor and compassion. When we can't be honest with the One who created us and knows what we're thinking anyway, then we'll have millions of miles to cover to get to the place where we can be honest with our loved one who didn't create us and doesn't have a direct line to our heart, mind, and emotions.

Plus, prayer centers the relationship on God and diverts focus away from self and onto your spouse—the perfect starting point for better, deeper communication.

10 Practical Tips for Better Communication

The process of communication involves three items: the message itself, the message sender, and the message receiver.

As mentioned, an average verbal message is comprised of content (i.e. the words used), tone of voice, and non-verbal cues. Maintaining consistency between all three aspects is a key ingredient to conveying a message that a receiver can fully understand. Of course, the content of what you say matters, but so does the way you verbalize it and the way the rest of your body communicates it. (Maybe this is why email is such a poor venue for intimate communication.)

Now, let's talk about strategies that a sender and a receiver can use to ensure that they're heard and understood.

1. A sender should be specific.

Proverbs 10:19 helps here: "When words are many, sin is not absent, but he who holds his tongue is wise." Using too many words during an important discussion can actually break down intimate communication. Carefully consider your words, seek clarity in your communication, and then share your relevant and specific thoughts, experiences, or feelings.

2. A sender should avoid exaggeration.

Prefacing judgments with "You always . . ." or "You never . . ." is a sure-fire way to produce backfire. When a sender opts to use broad or inflammatory language, the receiver will become defensive, quickly building a mental moat so they won't get burned.

3. A sender should be current.

In other words, they should discuss the "here and now" of the relationship and not "ancient history." Phrases like "I told you so," "How many times do I have to tell you?" and "When will you ever learn?" humiliate the other person and foster defensiveness. Furthermore, when a sender refers to other relationships with phrases like "I've never had this problem with someone else," or "My friends don't seem to have trouble understanding me," the sender creates a relational wedge that makes the receiver doubt the sender's commitment to the relationship.

4. A sender should be self-disclosing.

This goes back to Steps 4 and 5 on the levels of communication, where sharing one's feelings comes naturally. It's a "nakedness" of the soul that comes with risks, but better rewards. Such self-disclosure should always be appropriate in both quality and quantity, as Ephesians 4:29 reminds us: "Do not let any unwholesome talk come out of your mouths, but only what is helpful for building others up according to their needs, that it may benefit those who listen." Responsible self-disclosure brings healing, both to the sender and to the receiver. But negative self-disclosure is like a verbal enema—it's not fun and it hurts rather than builds up.

5. A sender should own their own feelings.

Closely related to self-disclosure, a sender must take responsibility for their own emotions. This takes self-discipline and a keen awareness of your own specific brokenness. Learning how not to blame others, even if they may have some culpability for a given situation, can be challenging, especially for those who've been hurt by a loved one. Even if your spouse did something terrible to offend or wound you, you are ultimately responsible for your feelings and your choice to react or respond. You might not be able to control your circumstances, but you can control your attitude.

Owning your own feelings encourages understanding because it's non-threatening. Those who learn how to take such ownership say, "I feel . . ." Rather than "*You made* me feel . . ."

6. A sender should use emotional word pictures.

Gary Smalley defines an emotional word picture as "a communication tool that uses a story or object to activate simultaneously the emotions and intellect of a person."[1]

Jesus's parables are emotional word pictures that have

48

engaged the minds and hearts of people for thousands of years. While you don't have to be as awe-inspiring as him, using emotional word pictures helps to cement our words into another person's heart.

Furthermore, they help couples find common ground for communication. Maybe one person can't think of specific "feeling" words to express their heart (typically true for many males), but they can tell a story that describes how they feel.

7. A receiver should be active.

Though it doesn't appear so on the outside, listening is an active skill. Effective listening requires that the receiver offer their full attention to the sender in order to truly hear what they're saying and understand what they mean and feel.

Active listening should be noticed by the sender. For instance, a receiver ought to look the sender in the eye, provide verbal feedback when necessary (even if only the occasional "uh-huh"), and use positive touch when appropriate.

Smart receivers also know when to dig deeper to see if there's an issue behind the issue at hand.

8. A receiver should postpone thinking about their response.

This common problem has existed for a long, long time. Proverbs 18:13 says, "He who answers before listening—that is his folly and his shame." A receiver shouldn't interrupt a sender,

---

and they also shouldn't be halfway focusing on the sender's words while also formulating their own response. For better communication to occur, the receiver needs to focus as much as they can on the sender's words, tone, and body language.

Furthermore, a receiver should accept what is said without *immediately* judging the content being discussed. James 1:19-20 reminds us, "Everyone should be quick to listen, slow to speak and slow to become angry, for man's anger does not bring about the righteous life that God desires."

9. A receiver should ask questions.

The best active listeners are those who ask questions at the right time in order to seek clarity or provide encouragement. Because they want to fill in as many blanks as they can, they ask questions to help themselves better understand the content and the sender's reasons for sharing that content. This is where we mirror back to the sender what we think we've heard them say.

In fact, active listeners often turn sender's statement into kind questions as a way to ensure they're correctly hearing and understanding what the sender's trying to say. For instance, a questioning receiver might say, "When you said you were angry at him, did you mean . . . ?"

10. A sender and a receiver should be patient with each other.
Here's the thing about this list. Though it was divided between sender and receiver, its audience is everyone. We ping-pong back and forth between sender and receiver thousands of times every day. Some of us are better at one or the other, but it's very likely that we all need help in at least one area.

As you begin to put into practice some of the strategies I've outlined above, be patient with yourself and your spouse. It may be awkward at first, but I guarantee that you'll witness surprising results as you both grow into better communicators.

* * *

Seeking to enhance your communication in marriage is one of the greatest acts of love you can show to your husband or wife. It means that you want your marriage to succeed, your children to have positive role models, and your spouse to see how much you value them.

Today, make one intentional change to your communication habits. Tomorrow, add another.

See if you might just begin to start dancing over what was once a landmine-filled war zone.

[1] *The Language of Love*, Gary Smalley, pg. 17

4

Fight Right

A CONFLICT-FREE marriage would be paradise, wouldn't it?

There's this couple who somehow managed *for fifty years* to have a conflict-free marriage. On the event of their fiftieth wedding anniversary, a local newspaper reporter asked them about their storied happy marriage.

"What's the secret behind your relationship's success? How have you both managed, for all these years, to be known as the town's most peaceful and loving couple?"

With a gleam in his eye, Tom glanced up at the young reporter.

"Well, it began very early, on our honeymoon in fact. We went to the Grand Canyon and took a coupla' horses to the bottom. We hadn't gone too far down when my wife's horse stumbled. She right near fell off the thing. I saw her give the horse a stern look, then she just said, 'That's once.' About a mile later, that horse lost its footing again and made Linda drop her water. She paused, gave the horse that same stern look, then said, 'That's twice.' Course, as that poor horse's luck would have it, he stumbled yet again. This time, my wife got off her horse, took a gun from her purse, then shot the animal!"

The reporter's eyes couldn't have gotten any wider. "What happened then?"

"I couldn't believe it! First off, I didn't know she had a gun. Second, I didn't know she knew how to use a gun. And third, I didn't know she'd kill a horse for bein' a horse. I shouted at her, 'What's wrong with you woman? Why'd you shoot that poor animal? Are you crazy?' She slowly gazed up at me with a look I'd seen before: 'That's once.'"

The reporter dropped his pen and paper. "Then what?"

"We've been happily married ever since."

Old Tom laughed, but the reporter couldn't tell if he'd been fooling around or not. He published the story as-is the next day, much to Old Tom's delight.

A Peaceful, Easy Marriage

OK, I'll admit it. That's a total pastor story. You know what a pastor story is? It's an embellished illustration pastors use to make a point. Sometimes they've really happened and sometimes not. Sometimes they become exaggerated as more and more pastors use the story, like a spiritual game of Telephone. Although I'd like to believe the story I just shared has some origins in truth, Tom and Linda's tall tale underscores this chapter's divisive topic: conflict.

I hate to break it to you, but your marriage will never be conflict-free. One person + one person = two perspectives, and two perspectives = inevitable conflict. Yes, there are healthy ways to deal with and mitigate conflict, but major differences of opinion will be a constant thorn in the side of *both* people in the relationship. Over time, you may even begin to believe that the other person *is* the thorn. The most difficult part about conflict in marriages is the fact that we're warring with the one we profess to love.

So, aside from the threat of horse-murdering violence, how can a man and woman in a covenant relationship fight without becoming enemies?

Conflict Can Be Good for You

Conflict is like dynamite. If used rightly, it helps people. Used wrongly, it kills.

Conflict is also like fire. It will burn you, but it'll also guide your way.

The key aspect in both of those illustrations is the

knowledge and experience of the one wielding the substance. If a person understands the constructive aspects of a destructive device, they'll be much more wary about its dangers and more intent on reaping its benefits.

If you know how to deal with it, conflict can actually benefit your marriage. In fact, conflict can push your marriage to new heights, but only if you allow it to be a sanctifying process and not a game you have to win at all costs.

I've been married to my best friend for almost forty years. We know about conflict. Over those decades, we've learned a few things about each other, but we've learned an immense amount about handling conflict well. Of course, neither of us is perfect, but we know now to look deeper than the surface issue that often gives way to conflict in our marriage. We ask ourselves questions like:

- Why did this happen?
- What's really at the heart of this issue?
- Where do *I* need to grow and change?

Essentially, we've learned that conflict can be holy and healthy once we get past the emotions of the moment and take an honest look at our own hearts. But that might be putting the cart before the horse right now, and we know what happens to horses in this chapter.

In the following pages, I'm going to dive into what typically causes conflict, our common reactions to it, what conflict reveals about us, and practical ways to handle conflict so that our marriages can thrive instead of take a dive.

What many may see as trouble in paradise could lead the both of you to a marriage you've never dreamed possible.

Our Major Causes of Conflict

Of course, conflict can erupt for all kinds of reasons, but these three particular reasons are often the deeper issues hiding just beneath the surface of many of our marital arguments.

Competing desires

James 4:1-2 says, "What causes fights and quarrels among you? Don't they come from your desires that battle within you? You want something but you don't get it."

This may be the broadest, most basic source of our conflict. The wife wants something; the husband wants something else. It's not rocket science, though seeking resolution in such instances can sometimes feel that way. Our varying needs and desires (see Chapter 2 for a refresher) will be a frequent source of conflict in our marriages.

It doesn't help that our culture constantly feeds us the lie of "have it your way" either.

Unresolved issues

These issues can come from outside or inside of the home. A husband may bring his work woes home with him, taking out his day-job anger on his wife. A wife may misunderstand something and think her husband made a derogatory remark about her, letting that unchecked thought fester into bitterness.

These are often problems that begin as the size of a snowball. As time passes, the snowball turns into an avalanche, claiming victims throughout a household. Unresolved issues don't melt away. They harden into anger, resentment, bitterness, and conflict.

Unmet expectations

This may be the most hurtful cause of conflict because the "victim's" hopes suffer a terrible blow.

Consider the new husband on his honeymoon, full of sexpectations, only to be met with a sunburned wife.

Or the new mom who's barely slept in a week as she waves goodbye to her husband heading out the door for a round of golf with the guys.

Or the empty-nesters with two totally different ideas as to what to do with all their free time.

This list is endless. We all bring certain expectations to our marriage, and for a wide variety of reasons. Having expectations isn't a bad thing, but having *unrealistic* expectations—and especially ones that are never communicated—will inevitably lead to at least one person spending the night on the couch.

Five Common Reactions to Conflict

When faced with conflict, most of us react in one of five ways. Depending on the situation, you may react in a few of these ways, but it's likely that you have a set (comfortable) pattern for responding to conflict. Read through these five reactions and identify your most common response.

1. My Way

Frank Sinatra sang it best. Unfortunately, his famous song could be an anthem for the fallen. Wanting it "my way" led to The Fall after all.

When we say, "I want it my way," what we mean is, "I want to win. I will not budge. You're obviously wrong. I'm obviously right. Why can't you see that?"

There's no grace in the "my way" method.

2. No Way

History would have us believe that ignorance is bliss, and the "no way" reactors believe just that. Desiring to seem less selfish than the "my way" reactors, they withdraw from conflict so they don't have to deal with it. They don't want to give in to the other person, and neither do they want to extend the battle. Consequently, they pretend as if the argument doesn't exist or matter. They falsely believe, "What I don't see can't hurt me."

There's no resolution in the "no way" method.

3. Give Way

Like someone who hesitates to enter the freeway, "give way" reactors always yield to others. Whether to gain acceptance or to quickly end the conflict, they always give in to the other person. Those who give up so quickly fool themselves into thinking they're bringing peace to the relationship since their conflict quickly disappears. However, these types of relationships can be especially unhealthy as one person's self-esteem erodes while the other's inflates.

There's no equal standing in the "give way" method.

4. Halfway

With two people in a marriage, it would seem to make sense to split who wins each argument. Compromise exists, but sometimes in a strange tit-for-tat way where one person gives way to the other because the other person gave way to them last time. Such reactions require a constant scorecard or record of accounts, which, let me remind you, is something Paul said love doesn't do (1 Corinthians 13:5). This method feels right because it seems egalitarian, but it combines the "give way" and "no way" methods I've already mentioned. Ultimately, it's an immature way to respond to conflict.

There's no lasting satisfaction or peace in the "halfway" method.

5. Our Way

Those who pursue "our way" work out their issues together. They not only care about solving the problem at hand, they also care about the other person and the relationship itself. That's not to say that those who tend to react in other ways don't care about their relationship or their spouses. It's just that those who react to conflict "our way" look at their spouse's needs and their own character instead of vice-versa. It's not about winning the argument; it's about restoring the relationship.

There's grace, resolution, equal standing, peace, and selfless love in the "our way" method.

The Heart Issues Conflict Reveals

When we're at war with another person, and especially if that person is our spouse, we tend to hate conflict. As seen in the list above, we often want to deal with it as quickly as possible so the relationship can revert to some semblance of peace and normalcy.

But I think there's a deeper reason why we want to get over

conflict so quickly. It exposes us and reveals what we work so hard to keep hidden. Though there are more, let's consider these three heart issues that conflict is so adept at unmasking.

Guilt

Guilt alters our emotional and spiritual states of being. It silences the still, small quiet voice of God speaking into our lives and causes one spouse to "hide" from the other, much like the guilt-ridden Adam and Eve hid from God at the dawn of time. The Psalmist describes guilt as "a burden too heavy to bear" which causes him to "groan in anguish of heart" (Psalm 38:4, 8).

Guilty people are typically depressed and depressing. Their emotional dryness can cause them to become distant and hard-hearted, causing a never-ending cycle of conflict, or at least low-level relational discord. Guilty people can also be highly defensive, making them capable of destructive blame-shifting, denial, and deflection. Because they often refuse to take responsibility for their own actions, they can also be harsh and judgmental. Lastly, they can be hypersensitive and fearful to trust others.

Guilt is a beast of a burden for anyone to carry, and it has the capacity to ruin relationships. So, when conflict reveals a guilty heart, what's the best way to cast off that burden? We'll get to that.

Selfishness

Like guilt, selfishness leads to a vast collection of unhealthy character traits: irritability, bitterness, greed, jealousy, and anger.

A selfish person lacks consideration for others, and nowhere is this more pronounced than in marriage. More often than not, selfishness reveals itself in conflict when one person fails to meet the other's expectations—even their *realistic* expectations. When one person demands that their expectations be met without conversation or compromise, that person is selfish.

This is completely antithetical to the way of Christ.

Paul's letter to the Philippians couldn't be clearer: "Don't be selfish; don't live to make a good impression on others. Be humble, thinking of others as better than yourself. Don't think only about your own affairs, but be interested in others, too, and what they are doing" (Philippians 2:3-4, NLT). Paul provided the answer to releasing yourself of the burden of selfishness, but we'll delve more deeply into how to do that at the end of this chapter.

Pride

Most people wouldn't publicly call themselves "prideful," though we're all guilty of being just that. Consequently, pride can often be challenging to identify. Outer signs of a prideful person include being argumentative, manipulative, overly critical, domineering, withdrawn, or super-religious. A person guilty of expressing any of these character defects may chalk it up to low blood sugar or just a bad day, but chronic instances of such actions reveal a much deeper and more sinister problem.

If you happen to be married to a prideful person, it's in your spouse's best interest that you find some tactful way to approach their sin. As Proverbs 16:18 reminds, "Pride goes before destruction, a haughty spirit before a fall." In refusing to acknowledge how pride might be destroying a relationship, spouses risk their marriage on the altar of comfort and perceived normalcy. However, a pride issue often requires God-led intervention into the life of the arrogant spouse.

Allow me to get in your face just a bit: if you read through the three major heart issues above and failed to identify yourself at all in any of the categories, you may have some work to do. I'm sure you're a nice person (you bought this book, which means you want to work for a better marriage, and I absolutely respect you for that), but we've "all fallen short of the glory of God," and our covenant marriages should strive as best as they imperfectly can to reflect his work in our lives. I've never met a person without at least a little baggage in one (or all) of these areas. So, if necessary, slowly re-read through the section above and remember to consider your character. You will never be able to fix your spouse, but you can definitely work on yourself.

Now to the good stuff.

How to Handle Conflict and Resolve Differences

As a pastor, I have a firm belief in tried-and-true multi-step programs. As long as a strategy for life change has three or seven steps (biblical numbers), I'm certain that it will solve all of your life's issues so long as you follow the steps as closely as possible.

I'm kidding.

Sorta.

I don't believe that a step-by-step strategy can instantly solve all of your issues, but I do believe that God can use a teachable, pliable heart to effect real and lasting life change in a person and in their marriage.

Plus, the following steps are all biblical, and God's word has *never* let me down.

1. Recognize the cause.

Ultimately, the cause is our fallen nature and our constant concern for our own selfish desires. More specifically, a husband and wife should do the hard work of discovering the root cause of their conflict. More often than not, the true cause isn't what the argument is actually about. As my marriage counselor used to say, "Often the issue isn't the issue." Meaning, the presenting issue is seldom the root issue. If you seek ways to resolve an argument but fail to discover the actual cause of the argument, you haven't resolved the actual conflict. It will just erupt again at a later date, and likely with more fury. If you only remove a weed at the surface, it tends to come back. It may be difficult to dig into the heart issues, but the health of your marriage may demand such hard work.

2. Listen to understand.

Speaking of causes for conflict, my attitude about my in-laws has sometimes made me an outlaw. When my wife once said something about my bad attitude, it ticked me off, and I made a stupid reply. (Shocking, I know.) During the ensuing game of verbal ping-pong, she finally said, "I don't feel like you're really listening to me." I paused and realized it was the first thing I'd actually heard her say during our argument. It was (another) wake-up call for me.

It never ceases to amaze me how effective honest, intentional, active listening can be. When you listen with the goal of sincerely understanding your spouse—without thinking up your rebuttal while they're still talking—you demonstrate honor for them and your desire to have a healthy relationship.

Furthermore, when you place your own needs and desires aside in order to actually hear and understand your husband or wife, you'll often discover a truth about the situation or about your relationship that can help lead you both to a meaningful resolution. Such active listening can help you recognize the real cause of the conflict and identify where you need to take responsibility.

3. Own your part.

I should say here that almost every step in this process takes courage. These suggestions buck against our selfish natures. We must often war with ourselves in order to bring peace to our relationships. Whether in the Middle East or in the middle of our marriages, conflict resolution is hard.

I think many Christians are keen on quoting Jesus's "Why worry about a speck in your friend's eye?" when *they're* the ones being judged. Too few of us, however, focus on the pointed, active verb he uses in the latter half of that command: "First, *get rid of* the log in your own eye."

Rather than blame, own. Instead of accusing, admit.

I've said this a gazillion times, and I'll never tire of saying it: being relational is more important than being right. When we make being right a greater concern than being relational, we're *wrong*.

When you own your part of the argument, you take the ammo out of the other person's gun. (Old Tom could have used that). Remember, Proverbs 15:1 says, "A gentle answer turns away wrath, but a harsh word stirs up anger." In taking responsibility for yourself, you're breaking the cycle of conflict and leading yourself and your spouse along a better path.

Owning your part requires honesty with yourself and with your spouse without shifting even an *iota* of blame onto your spouse (even if you really, really want to and they really, really deserve it).

It also means confessing your failure without minimizing what you did. Come clean with your mistake without *any* justification or rationalization. If you've rarely spoken such words to your spouse before, you may be amazed at how such raw transparency breeds the same in the other person, starting a better cycle of confession and forgiveness—much like a relationship with God. Confession can cure guilt too.

Also, conflict is *never* 100 percent the other person's fault. There's always something you can own.

4. Express hurt without hostility.

Unhealthy and unholy conflict hurts both people in the relationship. However, when dealt with in humility and godliness, each spouse should feel secure enough in their relationship to be honest about their feelings. The best way to prevent hostility from escaping out of the sides of your mouth is to shore up your speech with "I" messages rather than "You" messages. This is one area where being selfish, in a way, is recommended.

For instance, instead of saying "You made me mad when

you yelled at me," turn the phrase around to "I feel angry because of what happened yesterday." By placing the emphasis on your own feelings, you're ensuring that the other person doesn't feel threatened and become defensive. "You" statements are intimidating. "I" declarations help diffuse hostilities.

If anger or some other heightened emotion prevents you from being able to responsibly talk with your spouse, take a time out and pray to God about your hurt. He's big enough and trustworthy enough to take your anguish and turn it into something *better* rather than *bitter*.

5. Humble yourself.

As if the previous two steps weren't already humbling enough, this step requires a greater sacrifice than a hard discussion or owning up to a mistake. Humbling yourself means what I like to call "practicing otherliness." Because of the love we have for our spouses, we place their needs above ours and treat them as more important than we are (Romans 12:10). We lay down our rights to ourselves—like Christ did for the Church—in order to restore a right relationship (Philippians 2).

This doesn't mean that one person becomes a doormat for the other; rather, this is an intentional act of honor within healthy boundaries and with reasonable expectations.

Humbling yourself is the antidote to pride. Humble hearts beat in tune with God's heartbeat. "Humble yourselves before the Lord, and he will lift you (and your marriage) up" (James 4:10, New Revised Bubna Version)

6. Embrace contrition.

The three most powerful words in the English language are "I love you." But do you know the five most useful?

"I'm sorry. Please forgive me."

When spoken at the right time for the right reasons and with the right tone, these simple words bring order back to chaos. They shine light into darkness. They make whole what was cracking. They bridge a seemingly ever-increasing gap between two people. They heal.

And when a husband and a wife can both say these words in all sincerity to each other following a fight, something truly God-inspired has occurred.

7. Reaffirm your love.

Conflict is inevitable, so wise men and women should plan for it to sometimes wreak havoc on their marriages. No one wants to endure it, but as you've read, if handled correctly with the relationship placed above self, conflict can draw a couple much closer together. Successfully navigating the turbulent waters of conflict will also make you both that much better at resolving conflict the next time a storm comes to rock your boat.

Certainly, all of these steps are important *during* conflict resolution, but this last step is essential before, during, and after conflict. When two people both dispose of the divorce bullet from their conflict management arsenal, they're left with one option if the marriage starts heading south: they have to stick by each other. They must learn how to resolve their arguments and differences because the alternative leaves both people miserable for a long, long time.

When there's a deep and abiding commitment *by both parties* to the relationship that isn't solely based on "being happy" or conflict-free, then both people have an intense motivation to resolve conflict. Life's far too short to live it in misery. As often as possible, reaffirm your love for your spouse. Remind yourself why you fell in love in the first place. Choose to *grow* through conflict, not just *go* through it.

Be vocal with your love. Be generous with your praise. Be public with your honor. Problems will occur in your marriage, but with God's help and your cooperation, conflict can transform your relationship instead of destroying it.

And you won't have to sacrifice a horse to make it so.

Now let's move on to an area of marital conflict that should be one of marital bliss: sex. (I wonder how many of the guys will have read that chapter first.)

5

The Naked Truth

WHAT IS IT about discussing sex that turns us all into quiet, nervous teenagers?

I still remember a middle-aged couple that walked into my office almost a decade ago. They needed a referee for an argument they'd kept having over and over about their sex life. Before they even started talking, I warned them (just as I'm warning you now), "I'm not a sex therapist or a professional counselor. I'm just a pastor, and the best I can do is give you some pastoral advice." They assured me that that's exactly what they desired.

Then there was an awkward pause. There's always an awkward pause in these kinds of conversations. I waited, as I always do.

The husband looked at me, then looked at his wife, then blurted out, "Well, this is *your* problem. *You* ask him."

She proceeded to ask me a question I'd heard a hundred times over in dozens of different ways, which leads me to believe that the Church at large hasn't received clear teaching on the matter. I'm not assuming that I can offer the one-stop solution for her question, but I helped them—like I hope to help you in this chapter—discover better answers than the ones they probably had never received in the first place.

"What *does* the Bible allow in sex?"

Three Unsexy Caveats

First, I should mention I won't be covering the wide variety of sexual problems that plague our society, from impotence to sexual abuse to pornography and the like, and how those issues often radically affect the marriage bed. There are far too many to cover, and there are a great many helpful books to read if you or your spouse wrestle with particular issues. Instead of addressing the "what-ifs" and "what-abouts" that can get very specific, I want to provide you with a broad and biblically solid basis that will open the doors to your spouse's garden of delights. (Yes, that's corny, but it's Song of Songs too.)

Secondly, I've offered pastoral counsel to enough people to know that if you've been sexually or emotionally abused, discussing sex can be overwhelming if not impossible. I'm not insensitive to your struggle, and my prayer is for your healing in that essential part of your life. I firmly believe that God wants to redeem our *whole* lives, and that includes our sexuality. This chapter will not delve into the difficult issues of abuse. If you're currently suffering in an abusive relationship, please tell someone and seek qualified help.

Lastly, I make no apologies for blatantly discussing sex in the context of Christian marriage. God created sex! It's also incredibly fun. And, judging by the questions I receive from couple after couple in my office, the church has done a pretty poor job of communicating how great God-ordained sex is. If the Church is to be salt and light to the world at large, we must deal with this issue and teach God's truth.

So, let's be adults (at least for a moment) and talk about sex.

What Does God Allow When Married Couples Have Sex?

You'll notice a theme in this book. Whenever I ask what could be, I'll preface it with what shouldn't be. It's definition by way of antithesis. When we know what something isn't, it helps chip away our erroneous definitions to see what is. To that end, the Bible specifically forbids the following sexual acts: adultery, fornication, homosexuality, incest, rape, bestiality, and abuse.

While most teenagers would (sadly) understand most of those words, "fornication" isn't one that's commonly used in our culture. Fornication means sex outside of the bonds of a covenant marriage, which would include premarital sex and sex with a prostitute. Additionally, sexual and emotional abuse aren't specifically addressed in the Bible, but the core problems that lead to such abuse—domination, humiliation, violation—definitely are. Such acts are outside the bounds of selfless love for others, and especially for one's spouse.

So, how did I answer that inquiring couple? What *does* God allow in sex?

I answered, "Anything sexual that destroys or displaces the God-ordained relational aspect of covenant marriage and selfless love is sin . . . " They were less than satisfied with that answer, but they hadn't let me finish either.

" . . . *but* there are no mandatory requirements in the Scriptures regarding position, oral sex, or the use of vibrators."

If I recall correctly, their jaws dropped at my candor. I'm assuming they'd never expected *those* words to come out of my mouth.

I expanded on my response, reminding them that God created sex and is an infinitely creative God. As long as a married couple's sexual playfulness and creativity in the bedroom are God-honoring and mutually agreeable, they're free to roam each other's gardens any way they'd like. (OK, yes, I'm a bit uncomfortable even writing that, but now you have a glimpse into my life as a pastoral marriage counselor!)

After hearing this, the husband looked at his wife, she looked back at him, then he grabbed her hands and excused the both of them for a "sudden appointment."

Essentially, this is what that man and woman had learned, grasped, and wanted to immediately put into practice:

A creative God created sex, and *in the context of covenant marriage*, it is a *gift* from him that he wants you and your spouse to *enjoy* to the maximum.

God created you and your spouse and ordained your marriage so that you two can have exhilarating, unbelievable, and mutually satisfying sex. In fact, I believe Christians ought to have the very best sex in the world. In fact, of all people, we should be sexperts!

Yet sex is so often a source of conflict rather than joy in our marriages. Sex should be a soothing balm, not a wielded weapon. Sex should be a selfless gift to each other, not a reward for good behavior. Sex should be relational superglue, not Velcro. Unfortunately, all of us have at one time carried guilt, negative past experiences, or a bad attitude into bed with us, and this complicates our sex lives and frustrates our mates.

Your most important sexual organ is your brain. What you think and how you feel about sex will make all the difference to your sex life. So what can we do to set our minds right so that our sex lives and marriages benefit?

Three Keys to Mutually Satisfying Sexual Fulfillment

I want you to memorize these three words right now: attitude, atmosphere, and approach. These are the keys you can use to unlock the doors to, well, you know where by now. All three issues must be understood and enacted before seeing any noticeable growth in your sex life. (Again with the awkward phrasing, I know, but it's hard not to titter like a teen when just about every word you want to use for marital health corresponds to some innuendo.)

1. Develop the right *attitude* about sex.

One woman once told me about her earliest training in thinking about sex. Her mother wholeheartedly disapproved of sex and told her that men needed it, but she should expect for it to never be any fun for her. Consequently, that woman tolerated sex for the first several years of her marriage. She would respond quickly to her husband's desires, not to serve him, but to get the ordeal over with as soon as possible. Following the birth of their first child, the woman told her husband that she never wanted to have sex again because she hated it.

Can you imagine the kind of relational turmoil that caused?

Eventually, they sought help from a biblical counselor and discovered sexual wholeness for their marriage. But it's not just

78

our parents that may provide us with a negative view of sex. Our churches are just as guilty. I grew up in a church that *never* discussed sex, which indirectly communicated to me that sex must be evil and/or God doesn't care about sex. I'd be willing to bet that many thousands of Christians experienced the same kind of upbringing. When left with such a vacuum of information, we'll seek out answers anywhere we can, which is probably why so much of what I learned about sex came from other just-as-ignorant teenagers at my junior high school.

But God is intimately concerned with our sexual lives. He created us to be sexual beings. We aren't to be *only* sexual beings as our culture might suggest, but neither can we run away from our sexual natures. When God seeks to redeem, he seeks to redeem every part.

Toward that end, let me remind you that the most powerful sexual organ in your body is your mind. That's why having the proper *attitude* toward your spouse and his or her sexual needs is paramount to a healthy and mutually fulfilling sex life.

First, rest assured that sex *is not* dirty, evil, shameful, or inherently sinful. There are some of you reading this book that need to re-read that sentence and discuss with a trusted friend or counselor about *why* you think sex could be described in any of those ways. In other words, if what's supposed to turn you on in marriage turns you off, you should talk to someone about that before it threatens to ruin your relationship.

When performed within the bounds of a covenant marriage, sex glorifies God. It is a holy activity that ought to be accepted, experienced, and celebrated within your marriage without shame or guilt. In *The Living Bible Translation* of 1 Corinthians 6:20, Paul says, "Use every part of your body to give glory back to God." He created every inch of our bodies to serve particular functions, and when those parts do their prescribed job for the glory of God, it's worship.

Consider the first time (naked) Adam laid eyes on (naked) Eve. I guarantee you that his first thoughts weren't, "What am I supposed to do with her? Well, maybe she's a good cook?" If I had to guess, I'm willing to bet his thoughts were more along the lines of, "Thank you God for this beauty you've freely given me. She's impressive, and I'm in awe of your handiwork. Thank you." In other words, he was *very* attracted to her, but he didn't let that attraction terminate on his own desires. In that state of perfection, he knew from Whom every good and perfect gift came—and he worshipped.

Read this now and put it into practice later: it's OK to be sexy and sexually active in your marriage. That's one of the reasons God ordained marriage. Sex within marriage is sacred (which is also one of the reasons the Enemy tempts all of us so strongly in this area). For too long too many of us have misunderstood the *gift* of sex. When we have errant thoughts and misleading beliefs about the true role of sex in our marriages, our actions and emotions surrounding our sex lives will undoubtedly be affected for the worse.

True success as a hot and holy lover is only possible when we choose to see sex the way God does.

2. Create the right *atmosphere* for sex.

When it comes to sex, most men don't have green thumbs.

A healthy plant left in a dark room that's never given food or water will inevitably die. Regardless of how healthy the plant was before it was starved of attention and care, it will die. *Atmosphere* matters, and yet we men tend to forget this *all* the time. Or, like newlywed me at eighteen-years-old, we're completely oblivious to the fact, blinded by lust and overloaded with testosterone.

We covered this in Chapter 2, but Gary Smalley's apt quote bears repeating: most men are like microwaves, while most woman are crock pots. Men have a light switch, which may oftentimes seem like it's stuck in the "ON" position. Women are like fireplaces that require the right environment and materials for a spark to catch fire. Women tend to take *much* longer than men to warm up to being sexual. And, for the most part, men need to learn how to better create an inviting atmosphere for their wives.

A married man once told me that he just wasn't getting as much sex from his wife as he used to. He was visibly frustrated by it and couldn't understand why she didn't get turned on the way she had before. After discussing their relationship in more detail, I learned the reason why she'd turned cold on him. She wasn't doing what she used to because he wasn't doing what he used to!

The key fact is that she wasn't being *sexual* because he wasn't being *environmental*, so to speak.

When they were dating and during the first few years of their marriage, he'd *always* open doors for her. He'd help around the house. He'd call her for no other reason than to say he loved her. He did the little things that somehow seem to slip through the cracks of our daily lives the longer we're married. But it was these little things (in his mind) that led to the big things (in his mind). Collectively, these actions had stoked her fires all day long, so she was more than ready to burn for him at night.

The lesson for guys is one that Dr. Kevin Lehman immortalized in his book, *Sex Begins in the Kitchen*. While it *can* literally begin in the kitchen, that's not what he meant. When a man helps his wife in the kitchen, he's starting the timer on *her* crockpot. Women tend to be stimulated by romance, tenderness, loving acts of service, and *non-sexual* touch. They are responders, and that's OK.

Men don't work that way, so when a husband approaches his wife with the belief that she wants sex all the time (because he does), both will be disappointed. The husband's approach will be rebuffed, and he may have to attend to his emotional wounds for a few days before another attempt. The wife may feel like she's simply being used to meet his needs and may ultimately find sex distasteful. When she doesn't feel romanced, wooed, wanted, and special, she has little reason to give herself to her husband.

Above all, she must feel all-day affection, from the kitchen to the bedroom and everywhere in between. Romance ought *always* to precede sex. The sooner a man discovers that, the better his marriage's sex life will be. As for practical ways to regain those lost, loving feelings:

- Plan a regular date night and act like you did when you first dated.
- Be intentional about spending time together. Talk together, touch, and enjoy each other's company.
- Take walks together.
- Surprise her with a card, flowers, or a small gift.
- Call her for no other reason than to say, "I love you because . . ."
- Tell her how beautiful she is to you. (Women with body image issues may struggle with the nakedness that sex requires.)
- Be chivalrous. Open doors for her. Hold her hand in

public.

- Ask about her feelings and *listen* to what she says. (Emotional struggles can stall anyone's sex drive.)
- Serve her. (Fatigue negatively affects sexual fulfillment.)
- Kiss, hug, and touch her in non-sexual ways.
- Above all, directly *ask* her what she needs and likes for romance and how she would prefer to be treated by you.

Ladies, if you see your husbands making these attempts, don't point it out to him and don't make him feel bad about his past shortcomings. Some men may feel awkward about it because it's not "who they are," while others may feel guilty about the way they've treated you before. Realize that a husband working on adding more romance into your life is one who's committed to you and you alone. Be patient, provide positive reinforcement, and offer coaching every now and then on what works for you and what doesn't. In time, you should both notice a marked difference between your bedtime and your time in bed.

3. Practice the right *approach*.

By the "right" approach, I mean better and different than the "same old" approach you may take week after week and month after month. Don't worry, I'm not about to go Dr. Ruth on you and make us both uncomfortable. However, there are some great Christian books that get very specific about enhancing your bedroom techniques. What I want to briefly discuss are a few basic changes you can make in your approach to sex that can enliven your marriage's sex life.

First, be spontaneous. This might be a revelation to some, and especially to those chained to their calendars, schedules, and smartphones: you can have sex with your spouse *anytime* and *anywhere* (so long as it's wise and legal). But, guys, remember the last point we talked about. Spontaneity still requires preceding romance. And women, your husband will *greatly* appreciate a spontaneous encounter that you initiate. It doesn't have to be often—it wouldn't be spontaneous then—but allowing yourself to be sexually spontaneous with your spouse invigorates a marriage.

Next, get creative. I'm not suggesting anything pornographic, dirty, or degrading, which is what our world too often connotes with creativity in sex. I am suggesting that you learn what your spouse appreciates in bed, then discover creative ways to meet that need, always remembering that *everything* a married couple does in bed should be ultimately mutually satisfying. Creativity in bed prevents monotony from ruining monogamy.

Song of Solomon, a book of the Bible that young Hebrew boys were forbidden to read because of its graphic depiction of sex, describes how creative, innovative, and passionate sexual love can be:

"I am my lover's, the one he desires. Come, my love, let us go out into the fields and spend the night among the wildflowers. Let us get up early and go out to the vineyards. Let us see whether the vines have budded, whether the blossoms have opened, and whether the pomegranates are in flower. And there I will give you my love" (Song of Solomon 7:10-13, NLT).

Someone cue the Barry White!

She's talking about sex in the fields, a pretty creative way to spice up a love life. Now, be responsible in your creativity. I don't want you to hold this book up to the police officer when he asks you what you and your spouse were doing naked on the beach. But do consider how you can bring freshness to an area of your relationship that may have grown stale.

Lastly, communicate *a lot*. We've discussed how vitally important honest communication is between a husband and wife. Great sex finds its origin in great communication. In *60 Things God said About Sex*, Lester Sumrall keenly identifies the intimate connection between communication and sex: "I firmly believe that the men and women of America would have much more enjoyable sex lives if they would take the time to learn how to really communicate. A man who patiently learns the sexual language of his wife will always be ravished by her love. The woman who tunes her ear to her husband's sexual messages will be fully satisfied. But it takes time. It takes patience."

Far too many men and women suffer from "performance anxiety" with their spouse because they don't know if they're meeting their spouse's sexpectations. I'm going to offer you a shocking word of advice: just ask them about it. Yes, it might be awkward, but the ultimate reward is worth the momentary discomfort. In addition to asking honest questions, be sure to fearlessly share your own desires and needs too.

I've been married to the love of my life for four decades. We know what each other likes *because we tell each other about it*. Of course, this didn't happen on our honeymoon. In fact, it took us many years to arrive at a place of security and maturity where we could talk with each other about our sexual needs without feeling personally threatened. But what a difference good communication has made.

I cue the Barry White every night now. OK, every other night. (I'm sorry. As this chapter draws to a close, I had to make you uncomfortable at least one more time.)

Without the right attitude, atmosphere, and approach, sex in your marriage will be a to-do instead of a get-to-do, a worry instead of a joy, and a demand instead of a gift. God wants you and your spouse to *thoroughly* enjoy the good gift of sex.

Because when you don't, bad things happen.

6

When the Vow Breaks

THREE KINDS OF people must read this chapter: those who've had an affair, those who may be tempted to have an affair, and those who believe they're incapable of having an affair.

In other words, everyone.

For those who've been unfaithful, God's grace is still available to you. The words in this chapter can help ensure you don't make the same life-altering mistakes twice.

For those tempted to have an affair, the following words of warning will show you why that's one of the worst decisions you could ever make.

For those who believe they'd *never* enter into an adulterous relationship—and I hate to say this—your spouse might. I've heard about that happening more times than I'd like to admit. Very seldom is one spouse not utterly shocked by their spouse's admission of infidelity. Even if you're assured of your own faithfulness, sometimes it only takes one bad decision for a person to suddenly find themselves considering leaving their spouse. On a more positive note, reading this may be beneficial because you may one day be a biblical voice in the wilderness when a co-worker, friend, or family member admits to having an affair or suffers because of their spouse's betrayal.

It's challenging to talk about affairs without getting completely depressed. As a pastor who's counseled hundreds of couples suffering from infidelity, I've witnessed grown men weeping and adult women teeming with hatred. I've seen high school sweethearts become emotional cage fighters. I've heard deeply hurting husbands and wives let fly the choicest of nouns and adjectives in bitterness and pain.

It's not exaggeration when I say this: marital unfaithfulness shatters everything it touches. In the following pages, we'll discuss why we're prone to unfaithfulness, the anatomy of an affair, the essential practices you *must* put into place in your marriage to safeguard it from an affair, and how healing can be sought should an affair wreck your marriage.

This is a hard chapter to read, but you will serve your spouse, your marriage, your children, and God well by reading through it and carefully considering what next steps you may need to take so that your marriage doesn't become just another tragic statistic.

Why We Seek Out Affairs

Some reports say that 25 percent of men and 10 to 15 percent of women will have an affair during their lifetime. Read that statistic again. It should shock and sadden you as it does me. Plus, when asked if they'd have an affair if their spouse would never find out about it, many men and women said yes.

That breaks God's heart, and not only for the hurt spouse, but also for the one who commits adultery. Proverbs 6:32 shows why: "A person who commits adultery lacks judgment; whoever does so destroys himself." God doesn't want people destroying themselves or others, and even a cursory glance at the Ten Commandments reveals that truth. Of course, "Thou shalt not commit adultery" is one of those commandments, and with good reason.

If we've been told for ages that infidelity is so destructive, why does it seem like our society is so keen on promoting it? Why do our public figures, from celebrities and government officials to sports stars, seem to topple like dominoes because of affairs? Why do our churches seem so riddled with it as well?

It's an easy answer. We all want stew.

Though Genesis 25 doesn't tell the story of an affair (though there *are* many of those in the Bible), it relates a story of jealousy and betrayal, two issues at the core of every affair. To recap the longer story, younger brother Jacob desired older brother Esau's birthright, a special spiritual blessing given by a Jewish father to only his firstborn son that included the bonuses of a double portion of the family inheritance and the leadership mantle in worship and war. If you've read much of Genesis, you know this isn't going to happen, as God shows favor to younger sons over and over again. But the *way* it happens is fascinating.

Esau was a hunter and could have been cast as a stereotypical jock in a 1980s teen flick. His brother would have been the quiet, artistic introvert in the same film. When Esau arrived home one day, he acted like any teen, shouting to anyone in the vicinity, "I'm starving!" (despite the fact that he'd probably eaten less than a few hours ago). Jacob just so happened to be cooking stew at the time, and being a bit brighter (and more manipulative) than his brother, replied, "First sell me your birthright."

Esau, ever the teenager, replied, "I'M DYING HERE. What good is my birthright if I'M DYING, you moron?" (Genesis 25:32, New Revised Bubna Translation). Jacob told him to swear to it, and Esau, intoxicated by stew, swore his birthright to his younger brother.

The Bible uses an interesting word to mark this occasion: "So Esau *despised* his birthright." That means he was indifferent about the immense amount of gifts promised to him if only he could be patient enough to wait for them. To satisfy his momentary physical need, he relinquished what would have been long-lasting gain and reward.

He sacrificed his future for temporary pleasure. He gave up so much in return for so very little.

Do you see now how this story reveals the heart issues at play when an affair happens?

How to Have an Affair in Ten Easy Steps

It's tragic, but not many people need training in how to have an affair. For the most part, we can turn on a TV show or watch a film and figure out what steps we could take to go from Point A to the Point of No Return. But infidelity existed long before moving pictures. We don't need training in how to let our hearts wander from their first love. It's an unfortunate and intrinsic part of our nature, a remnant from the first time humans turned their backs on their true love.

Here's how affairs tend to happen. Whatever you do, *don't* follow these steps unless you absolutely want to ruin your life and the lives of those close to you. An unfaithful person is a suicide bomber on a mission where they don't know they're the weapon. And the blast radius is immense. When you find yourself falling into any of the patterns below, please, please, please consider telling a trusted friend, family member, or pastor about your struggle. The sooner you can admit to what's going on in your heart, the sooner you can prevent catastrophe.

Step 1: Ignore all reasonable and wise boundaries with the opposite sex. Go out for coffee "as friends" or take a "working lunch" with that attractive co-worker down the hall. Spend as much time as you can with this "friend."

Step 2: Flirt because it's fun and harmless. Use flattery and sprinkle in sexual innuendos.

Step 3: Linger when "accidental" physical contact occurs. Find reasons for it to occur more often.

Step 4: Share your deepest fears, thoughts, and feelings, especially those things you feel like you can never talk about with your spouse. Convince yourself that your "friend" understands you so much better than your spouse.

Step 5: Fantasize about what "it" would be like.

Step 6: Keep the relationship hidden as much as possible.

Step 7: Complain about your spouse as much as possible to your new "friend." Compare your "friend's" strengths to your spouse's weaknesses. This is the most important step to cementing your new relationship as better than your old relationship.

Step 8: Rationalize your new romance as true love. Spiritualize it by convincing yourself that you married the wrong person and God has now brought the "right" person into your life. Silence your critics with that God-card.

Step 9: Surround yourself with friends, films, and books that say it's perfectly normal to follow your heart.

Step 10: Stop listening to that still small voice of God's Spirit warning you against running away, and of course, don't pay any attention to the cautionary statements made by others either.

If you religiously follow these ten steps, I guarantee that you'll have an affair in no time. Sure, you may have fun for a while— hot stew after a long day is delicious after all—but you will sacrifice so much more than you'd ever considered possible. You will lose your marriage, your self-respect, a healthier future for your children, likely half of your friends, your peace, your true joy, your money, maybe your standing in the community or your reputation at work, and the respect of your family and friends.

As terrible as those losses are, none may be more terrifying than the possible loss of your faith.

While God draws near to the brokenhearted, don't be surprised if he goes quiet in your sin. In fact, the Bible equates unfaithfulness with walking into certain death: "With persuasive words she [an adulterous woman] led him astray; she seduced him with her smooth talk. All at once he followed her like an ox going to the slaughter, like a deer stepping into a noose till an arrow pierces his liver, like a bird darting into a snare, little knowing it will cost him his life" (Proverbs 7:21-23, NIV).

So how can we steer clear of walking like a deer into a noose?

How Not to Have an Affair

It is both possible and wise to remain in a monogamous and faithful relationship with your spouse. Our culture would have you believe otherwise, but our God is much bigger and wiser than our collective human wisdom. To do so, however, requires intentionally putting into place these vitally important practices, many of which I've learned from pastors like Rick Warren, Jack Hayford, and my friend Joe Wittwer.

1. Meet unmet needs.

When you're not meeting your mate's basic and reasonable needs, you're opening a door for them to experience temptation. You're inadvertently turning them into ripe fruit that won't take much movement to fall off of a tree. In my decades of experience with people, these unmet needs are often due to ignorance rather than blatant selfishness. Men and women alike just aren't that great at effectively communicating their needs and desires to each other. (See Chapter 3 for more help.)

For many women, their largest unmet need is generally emotional in nature. They desire affection and conversation as signs that their man cares for them. That's why so many women who fall into adulterous relationships begin their affairs through an emotional attachment with the other man. Since they're not having those needs met at home, they find someone who will meet those needs. This isn't always the case, but it happens quite often.

On the other side of the emotional spectrum, a man's largest unmet need is physical in nature. Simply put, they want sex. To them, the physical act equals emotional acceptance. Men typically enter into affairs because of their lust for the other woman and because their sexual needs aren't being met at home. Though exceptions occur, this is the norm for most male-initiated affairs.

The Bible speaks to both sexes on this subject. In 1

Corinthians 7:3, Paul says, "The husband should fulfill his marital duty to his wife [affection, conversation, emotional interest, etc.], and likewise the wife to her husband [physical touch, sex, etc.]." What we need to understand about each other is that these are legitimate needs for both sexes. Affair after affair that is confessed to me as a pastor can be traced back to failures in these two specific areas.

God's plan in marriage is simple: love and serve each other in such a way that your marriage brings *fulfillment* to *both* partners. When you do the hard and sometimes awkward work of ensuring that this happens, you protect your marriage from outside influences and destructive temptations.

2. Seek to resolve unresolved conflict.

We've already discussed how unresolved conflict can inhibit communication, but it also causes stress in a relationship, driving a distancing wedge between a wife and husband. Unresolved issues often lead to emotional and/or physical avoidance of the other person. Such withdrawal over time leads to bitterness and resentfulness. During those times, the Enemy who prowls around like a roaring lion may place someone in your life who just so happens to be of the opposite sex and "totally gets you." Because a void exists in your life that your spouse used to fill, you'll naturally gravitate toward someone who seems like an adequate and "temporary" replacement.

The only time you should *ever* talk about the problems in your marriage with someone of the opposite sex is if that person is a professional marriage counselor. As we read in Chapter 4, resolving conflict is difficult and demanding—but worth it. Don't wait until you hate your spouse to get help. Don't withdraw so much that your spouse becomes your roommate. Don't let bitter roots burrow into your soul. Seeking help, and especially at the earliest signs of distress, is the mature, smart, and godly thing to do.

There was a time in our marriage when Laura and I kept having conflict after conflict over the same issues. Like constant waves cutting into steep cliffs, the arguments eroded our relationship. Eventually, we didn't like each other all that much. Our marriage was adrift, as if we'd both been tossed into the sea and had floated impossibly far away from each other. A caring friend finally threw me a life preserver when he simply asked, "Have you guys seen a counselor?"

Why would a pastor need a counselor? I thought.

I'm kidding. I knew we needed help, and I was man enough to admit it. Plus, I missed my wife, wanted our marriage to thrive, and wanted to see God glorified through it all as well. So we went to counseling. And then we went again. And again. And again. It wasn't quick, but it gave us a future together. It wasn't easy, but it was essential. It wasn't how I always wanted to spend my time, but looking back I wouldn't have traded that season for anything else.

Asking for help in your marriage is not an admission of defeat; it's a courageous act done by those who want something more for their covenant relationship. (Please read that last line again, slowly.)

3. Control your thoughts.

Pastor Rick Warren succinctly makes this point: "Adultery begins in the head long before it gets into bed." The way you think determines the way you feel, and the way you feel determines what you do. The longer you think (fantasize) about doing something, the greater the likelihood you'll commit that act. Visualization can be helpful and hurtful; it just matters what you're visualizing. And we're often better at visualizing what's close, achievable, and desirable over what's far, difficult, and necessary.

Jesus understood this struggle and warned us about the direct link between our thoughts and actions. "You have heard that it was said, 'Do not commit adultery.' But I tell you that anyone who looks at a woman lustfully has already committed adultery with her in his heart" (Matthew 5:27-28).

Let's discuss the pivotal word in that command: lust. Lust is not attraction, appreciation, admiration, or arousal. God wired men and women to be attracted to each other, so it's natural for attraction to occur, but those *thoughts* and *feelings* are not lust.

Lust is what you *do* with those thoughts and feelings. It lingers on the second look and mentally undresses the other person. It fantasizes about "What if . . . ?" and compares the other person to your spouse. Lust plans a sexual encounter.

Thoughts and feelings of attraction transform into lust when those thoughts and feelings become sexual in nature and you dwell on them. Don't feel guilty because you're attracted; rather, learn to control and discipline your thought life.

Lust is a ravenous lion who's never satisfied. The more you feed it, the more it demands until it's taken all it can from you. By taking your thoughts captive and redirecting them to your spouse, you'll starve the lion of lust. By no means is it an easy task, but God gives grace to the willing and humble.

I've found that diverting my mind to prayer helps, even admitting to God the present struggle I may have when thinking thoughts I shouldn't be thinking. I remind myself that I committed my love to my wife. I wonder what my kids would think of me. I consider the people I lead at my church and my own standing before God—not that He'd forsake me—but that He'd go quiet on me. I remember the pain I've brought on myself through past mistakes. I weigh the grave cost that such a path would lead me to ultimately pay. By the time I've reflected on all of this, my momentary bent toward lust has passed.

I refuse the stew for the better reward.

4. Guard your heart.

"If you don't want to get stung, Kurt, stay away from the bees." That's what my mom used to tell me all the time. Because of an early bad experience with a wasp, my life's mission as a child was to destroy their nests whenever and wherever possible. The thing is, I'd still get stung. Little did I know how apt an illustration that would be for our temptation toward sexual sin. If you don't want to get stung by sexual sin, stay away from what will inevitably sting you!

Paul's letter to young Timothy emphatically warns him against even getting near to such dangers: "Run away from anything that stimulates youthful lust" (2 Timothy 2:22). Now's a good time to recall what we've already covered: what we think and dwell upon is often what we ultimately do. When it comes to sexual sin, when we allow our thought life to become polluted by the pervasive perversions of the world, it's not long before we try to hide behind a smokescreen of lies to cover up our sins.

God offers a prescription for that disease. In fact, it's preventative medicine that helps free us from future pain. Proverbs 4:23-27 says, "Above *all* else, *guard your heart*, for it is the wellspring of life. Put away perversity from your mouth; keep corrupt talk far from your lips. Let your eyes look straight ahead, fix your gaze directly before you. Make level paths for your feet and take only ways that are firm. Do not swerve to the right or the left; keep your foot from evil" (emphasis added).

"Guarding your heart" doesn't mean living in a bubble and physically running away at the sight of every attractive person of the opposite sex. It means establishing and maintaining healthy boundaries with the opposite sex in order to protect yourself and your marriage. To start your gears turning as to how you can specifically guard your heart, consider these situations that should warn your heart and mind to make a hasty retreat:

- Being alone in a private place with an unrelated member of the opposite sex.
- Being alone with someone with whom you have an obvious and unhealthy attraction.
- Lingering and/or inappropriate physical contact.
- Unhealthy and unholy media input, like smutty romance novels or sex-centric movies and TV series (Matthew 6:22).
- Emotional/physical weariness leading to moral failures.
- Hanging out in tempting places.
- Hanging out with bad company (1 Corinthians 15:33).

We all have hearts bent toward foolishness, and it only takes a spark to start a fire. However, when you actively work to purify your thought life, you're ensuring that no flames start burning for anyone other than your spouse. Stop for a moment and consider what areas of your thought life need purging. Talk to a trusted friend, pastor, or counselor about your issues. Let me remind you again that seeking help is a sign of courage, not weakness. Remember too that a very wise man once said, "God's power is made perfect in our weakness" (2 Corinthians 12:9). God is there for you in the midst of your struggle. Run to his throne with confidence, so that you may receive mercy and find grace in your time of need (Hebrews 4:16).

The grass is never greener on the other side unless the other side receives as much care and attention as your own. As you guard your heart, you're watering your own lawn, and you will see your marriage grow and thrive. When a marriage springs into full bloom, biblical phrases like "Let my beloved come into his garden and taste its choice fruits" take on an intoxicating, alluring, affair-preventing meaning (Song of Songs 4:16b).

It's far too easy for people today to have affairs, and our churches shouldn't be so riddled with infidelity and unfaithfulness. But we are all broken people in desperate need of a Savior on a day-by-day basis.

If you're in the midst of an affair right now, please carefully consider the cost of your actions. God still loves you, but the road before you will be immensely difficult, regardless of which path you choose. I pray you choose the right course, for yourself, your spouse, your children, your family, your friends, and most importantly, your relationship with God.

"The Lord is slow to anger and filled with unfailing love, forgiving every kind of sin and rebellion" (Numbers 14:18, NLT). That verse is from *Numbers*, which means it's been around for a long, long time. God has always been a forgiving God and desires to reconcile with you the same way he desires you to reconcile with your spouse. It won't be easy, but it will be worth it.

Give up the stew for the better reward.

But what if you've suffered as a result of an affair? What if you've been abused and had to leave your spouse out of fear for your life? What if you're one of the millions who've cited "irreconcilable differences" on their divorce decree? If God "hates divorce" (Malachi 2:16), does he hate you?

First, he doesn't hate you at all. There is nothing you could ever do to make God love you any more or any less than he already does. But he hates divorce because of what it does to the people he so deeply loves.

Second, whether you're the forsaken or the forsaker, let me encourage you to carefully read Chapter 8 on forgiveness. Healing is possible because the restoration of broken hearts and lives is God's specialty.

For now, let's dive into the tough and sometimes controversial subject of divorce.

7

The Scarlet D?

YOU ALREADY KNOW that my parents divorced each other after twenty years of marriage. It was difficult for everyone involved, as divorces always are. The negative effects rippled for decades, and some ripples may never find their resolution, but I'm glad to report that God was merciful to our family and to my parents. Eventually, they both experienced the healing and redemptive work of God in their lives. That's my family story, and I could tell you hundreds more just like it.

But I'm willing to bet you don't need me to.

The statistics regarding the increase in divorce during the 20th-century are shocking. Though the divorce rate has declined in recent decades (probably due to the increase in couples cohabiting), you or someone you know well has suffered a divorce. You have your own stories to tell, or you could tell me stories about other people in your life who are divorced.

Rice University sociology professor Michael Lindsay said, "Divorce is a cancer that is eroding the social fabric that holds our culture together." It's unfortunate that a Christian marriage book has to include a chapter on divorce, but it's a rampant problem in our society *and* in our church. Plus, the devastation divorce causes has far-reaching and long-lasting effects that forever alter many different lives—and not just the two seeking the divorce.

We need a proper understanding of God's take on divorce, why Jesus allowed it in specific instances, how to prevent it from happening in our marriages, and how to seek healing after a divorce has occurred. In discussing this oftentimes delicate topic, we must refrain from going to either of two extremes. The Bible doesn't allow for outright permissiveness, where we can do whatever we want because that's what we desire. But neither does it encourage rigid legalism, which is a harshness that dooms people for life. When we allow for permissiveness, we negate the authority of God's word, which *does* prescribe how best we ought to live. But when we become judgmental and dogmatic, we negate the abundant grace and redemptive mercy that God provides to all. We must look at all of the aspects surrounding divorce through dual-lensed glasses of grace and truth.

Why "The Big D" is a Big Deal

Divorced or not, you need to know and understand this right now: divorce is never God's plan, but it's also not an unpardonable sin. God does not see a scarlet letter "D" permanently attached to your soul. He's covered that with scarlet of his own. If you've been divorced, you do not have to live in dishonor for the rest of your days, though it may feel that way for a time as you seek healing. Forgiveness can be found (and we'll talk about that in detail in the next chapter).

So if God's grace ultimately covers the sin of divorce, why is divorce such a big deal?

Sin is always a big deal to God because it separates us from his purpose and plan for our lives. But we're often quite adept at minimizing our sin—even the so-called "biggies." Eventually, we realize that God's still small voice has been "stiller" than usual. Without confessing our sin and taking responsibility for our actions, we distance ourselves from God. Think about this for a moment: if God is unchanging and never moves, then who's moved when he feels far away?

Divorce is a big deal because it destroys all kinds of relationships. Obviously, former spouses suffer, but so do their children, and often for years on end after the divorce. Relationships with extended family members become strained depending on the circumstances leading up to the divorce.

Friendships fall away as sides are taken.

Divorce is also a big deal because God's Word is clear about his take on the subject. I'm willing to bet he knew from the dawn of creation that his most prized possessions would consistently fall short in their relationships. As the maker of marriage, he gets to define its boundaries, and the clear words Jesus spoke about divorce and remarriage serve that purpose while also allowing room for grace in relationships that break beyond mending.

Now let's take a look at what Jesus said about marriage, divorce, and remarriage.

What the Bible Says about Divorce

In Matthew 19, the Pharisees asked Jesus, "Is it lawful for a man to divorce his wife for any and every reason?"

Before we go any further, there are a few issues you should know about that prompted their question. First, divorce was rampant in Jesus's day, particularly among religious leaders too. In other words, not much has changed. Secondly, the Pharisees purposely phrased their question that way because of an internal squabble that two Pharasaic schools of thought were having at the time. The school of Shammai taught that the Deuteronomy 21 passage, where Moses allows them to issue a bill of divorce, only applies to *adultery*. The liberal school of

Hillel taught that divorce could be *for any reason*, even a burnt dinner. It should also be noted that both schools generally limited the right of divorce to the husband alone. Lastly, the alternative to quietly divorcing a woman or man caught in adultery in the Old Testament, according to the book of Numbers, was to be stoned to death. So, in Jesus's day, divorce was a popular and preferred alternative to capital punishment.

In other words, it was a loaded question from the Pharisees.

But as he so often did, Jesus didn't give in to one party or the other. He offered a third way that seeks to restore and redeem, and to provide an ultimate cure instead of a temporary band-aid.

Divorce is never God's plan.

"'Haven't you read,' he replied, 'that at the beginning the Creator "made them male and female," and said, 'For this reason a man will leave his father and mother and be united to his wife, and the two will become one flesh?' So they are no longer two, but one. Therefore what God has joined together, let man not separate'" (Matthew 19:4-6).

In these few words, Jesus said much. Using the same books of the law that the Pharisees revered, Jesus referred to the Genesis creation narrative, reminding them that God's plan for marriage has never changed. God intends every marriage to be permanent. Divorce is *never* God's plan. When the Ultimate

Authority of our lives joins two people together in marriage, it's supposed to be for life, in sickness and in health, for richer or for poorer, till death do you part.

Jesus also reminded the Pharisees that God made man and woman in his own image. That is, marriage is to be a living expression of his own communal nature, authority, and character. Marriage is also an illustration of Jesus's relationship with the Church. God constantly refers to the Church at large as his bride. A good and godly marriage reminds the world how precious lost humanity is to God.

So if marriage has such high aspirations, especially in the Church, why does divorce still run wild?

God Hates Divorce.

The Pharisees continued their questioning: "'Why then ... did Moses command that a man give his wife a certificate of divorce and send her away?' Jesus replied, 'Moses permitted you to divorce your wives because your hearts were hard. But it was not this way from the beginning'" (Matthew 19:7-8).

Whenever we turn our backs on God's way, it's most often because we've allowed our hearts to become calloused. Hardened hearts lead to hard circumstances, and we're more prone to committing sins when we refuse to let God penetrate our hearts and minds with his better way.

All divorce results from sin at some level and by someone; it is a spiritual and relational failure by one or both parties in the marriage. And God *hates* sin. This is why He's so blunt about divorce through the prophet Malachi: "So guard yourself in your spirit, and do not break faith with the wife of your youth. 'I hate divorce,' says the Lord God of Israel, 'and I hate a man's covering himself with violence as well as with his garment,' says the Lord Almighty. So guard yourself in your spirit, and do not break faith" (Malachi 2:15b-16).

God does *not* hate the divorced. He hates the act of divorce because of the destruction it brings to his creation and his plan. He hates what it does to the people he loves. In Malachi's day and age, a man who "covers himself with violence" referred to a warrior just returning from battle, covered in blood from gory hand-to-hand combat. (Who among the divorced doesn't feel like they've been in a drawn-out emotional and bloody war?) Essentially, God uses provocative imagery to make his point. He hates divorce because of the violent mess it makes in people's lives.

... But God Allows for Divorce Under Specific Circumstances.

After reminding the Pharisees of God's intention for life-long marriage and recalling Moses's permission to allow divorce, Jesus sets the standard for when divorce is allowed.

"I tell you that anyone who divorces his wife, except for

marital unfaithfulness, and marries another woman commits adultery" (Matthew 19:9).

In other words, divorce is allowed—but not mandated—in the case of marital unfaithfulness. God made a biblical provision for divorce when one or both partners in the marriage commit adultery. Why is this? Because God has the deepest knowledge of the value of *covenant*. He understands how challenging it is, especially for his imperfect creations, to continue their relationships when adultery has shattered trust.

To be clear, adultery is marital unfaithfulness in the form of any physical act of infidelity. It primarily refers to sexual misconduct involving any deviation from clearly defined biblical standards, including adultery, prostitution, homosexuality, pornography addiction, incest, or bestiality. These acts are a betrayal to the marriage covenant that destroys the "one flesh" bond.

Some readers (especially men) may be surprised to see pornography in this list. After all, it's not a sexual act that requires another person, and some would justify their behavior as "not hurting anyone." I beg to differ, and I think Jesus would have included pornography addiction in the list of acts that betray the marriage covenant. Note that I purposefully added the qualifier of "addiction" because no man has ever been free of occasional lust, and rare is the male who's never viewed porn. It's the addictive aspect of consistent pornography use that can ultimately ruin a marriage.

Why would Jesus have included it? The Greek word he uses in Matthew 19:9 for "unfaithfulness" is *porneia*, a broad term referring to sexual sin. *Porneia* is the origin of our modern-day word for pornography. Additionally, Jesus's words in the Sermon on the Mount are clear: "You have heard that it was said, 'You shall not commit adultery.' But I tell you that anyone who looks at a woman lustfully has already committed adultery with her in his heart" (Matthew 5:27-28).

For a woman, her husband's porn addiction is a grave breach in the mental, emotional, and spiritual bond with her husband, a real betrayal of their covenant. A woman wants deep and monogamous intimacy with her husband's heart and mind as well as his body. This is why most women have no qualms about pornography addiction being included in this list. But men, because they're wired differently and tend to compartmentalize their lives, believe they can prevent one "secret" area of their lives from influencing other areas. That's one of the reasons they'd argue *against* including porn addiction in the list. Yet I stand by my belief that it should be included because of the devastation it ultimately causes. It's a deep breach of trust often made worse for its long-term hiddenness. Additionally, pornography addiction is not always a man's issue, and women can be drawn to other forms of pornography that can be just as damaging to a covenant relationship. In other words, I'm saying that a divorce can be sought should one spouse betray the other through an addiction to pornography.

But here's an extremely important yet hard teaching: Jesus makes an *allowance* for divorce, but does not *demand* that it occur. Restoring shattered trust in the aftermath of unfaithfulness is one of the most grueling tasks a married couple can undertake—but it *can* be done, and the spiritual and relational fruits of such labors are incredible. God can take absolutely anything we give him, even a lifeless, hard-hearted, broken marriage, and bring restoration and reconciliation. As I have repeatedly stated, restoration is God's specialty.

For instance, I once knew a couple whom the world, and even the Church, would have said should have gotten divorced. The man had committed multiple affairs with other men *and* had contracted AIDS. Through many admissions, tears, and untold pain in both of their lives, the wife *forgave* her husband, and their marriage survived and eventually thrived. That's God at work, and that's why Jesus didn't mandate that a divorce *must* occur when infidelity does.

But he gives grace where grace is needed.

What the Bible Says about Remarriage

When asked, "Under what circumstances may a couple divorce and remarry and it's not considered sin in God's eyes?" I answer, "Adultery, abandonment, or abuse." As we've read, Jesus makes clear his concession to divorce in cases of adultery. In 1 Corinthians 7:15, Paul adds abandonment by an unbelieving spouse as another viable reason to allow divorce, so long as it's initiated by the unbelieving spouse. As the believer in the relationship, you are not to seek the divorce, but work to reconcile. Physical and emotional abuse aren't specifically covered in the Bible as a just cause for divorce, but the underlying issues that destroy these types of horrific marriages certainly are. Keep the big picture in mind: the biblical allowance for divorce is the serious breach of a marital covenant relationship. Anyone who has suffered abuse will tell you how destructive it is and how difficult it is to ever trust their spouse. So I consider abuse an allowable reason (though, again, not a mandatory one).

So when is a divorced person biblically free to remarry?

- If the divorce was due to adultery or sexual immorality and the marriage is dissolved, the innocent party is free to remarry without sin (Matthew 19:9).
- If the divorce was due to abandonment by an unbelieving spouse, the believer is free to remarry (1 Corinthians 7:15).
- If the divorce was due to serious and ongoing emotional or physical abuse, the wounded party is free to remarry.

- If the divorce was due to *any other reason*, the biblical standard is reconciliation with your spouse or remaining unmarried.

That last line is where people begin to get nervous, but Paul couldn't have been more clear about it in 1 Corinthians 7:10b-11: "A wife must not separate from her husband. But if she does, she must remain unmarried or else be reconciled to her husband. And a husband must not divorce his wife."

Why are these verses so hard for so many? Because hard hearts have a hard time allowing God's chisel to sculpt them into an honest husband or a forgiving wife or vice-versa. God doesn't make it easy for us to divorce because he *wants* us to do the challenging work of building and maintaining healthy marriages.

What God's straightforward command means is that a person cannot seek divorce on the grounds of:

- Irreconcilable differences
- Sickness
- Income
- Boredom
- Infertility
- Life's difficult circumstances
- A lousy sex life

- Unhappiness
- A belief that you married the wrong person

I'm not saying that these issues are easily handled. They definitely bring incredible amounts of stress to a marriage, but none that aren't common to marriages across the world. What I am saying is that God's standards are challenging because he takes marriage so seriously. He set these standards in place to protect us and the sanctity of the marriage covenant. Because he knows the hearts he set within us, he knows what's best for our lives. So much about the Christian life is learning to trust his authority in our lives, and our marriages are fertile ground God can use to bring about incredible spiritual growth, if only we'll trust and do what he says.

But what if you've been divorced for any other reason? Are you now relegated to the scratch-and-dent pile of life, and of no further use to God's Kingdom? Does God still love you?

How the Church Should Respond to the Divorced

Yes. A thousand times yes, God still loves you. If you've been divorced and have remarried for any of the wrong reasons I've just stated, know that there is still mercy and grace for you, but it requires something from you. When God's word has been violated, the only solution is confession and forgiveness.

Though adultery, abandonment, abuse and other issues that lead to divorce are considered "biggies" when it comes to sin (because of the wide devastation they cause), they are also sins that have been covered by Christ's work on the cross.

Divorce is *not* the unpardonable sin. If you earnestly seek God's forgiveness, forgiveness will be granted. You can live free from guilt and shame. The last chapter will take a detailed look at the process of forgiveness, and while everyone can benefit from reading it, I heartily encourage those who have suffered from divorce for any reason to read it and apply it.

One more thing: whether you've committed the sin of divorce or you've been sinned against, you will need time and help to heal. Find a Christian support group or a divorce recovery group and willingly dive into the process of renewal. Move slowly. Get help.

And please don't just jump back out there looking for love in all the wrong places—or even the right places—too soon.

Unfortunately, there are still many churches today that treat divorced people as second-class Christians. They fail to practice the forgiveness they preach. They forget Jesus's merciful interactions with the woman at the well in John 4, or the consistent, grace-full way he treated outcasts and prostitutes. Jesus verbally and physically illustrated God's unrelenting standard coupled with his relentless grace. The Pharisees of his day had a difficult time understanding it, as we often do today too. We want to judge others but exonerate ourselves.

In regard to marriage, divorce, and remarriage, the Church must ask itself a simple question: "Who do we want to look more like: the Pharisees or Jesus?"

Let's start looking more like Jesus, one who preached an unbending, unmovable, and absolute standard, but consistently and widely offered healing and grace to all who would seek it. And one of the best ways we can start looking like him is to learn how to truly forgive ourselves and others.

8

Hope for the Hurting

"I'LL GET TO it tomorrow."

Sarah cast a doubting glance at her husband. She'd heard that line before. She was pretty sure she'd heard it every day for the last month. Every time they crossed the bridge over the rushing creek in their backyard, she was sure it was going to give way. And every time they successfully made it to the other side, she'd start to say something to David, only for him to cut her off with, "I'll get to it tomorrow." If she wasn't so worried about actually getting hurt during one of their daily walks, she'd think their interactions were almost funny. But she knew that if the bridge didn't get fixed soon, both of them might get injured, a real danger that her husband was either ignorant of or just didn't care about.

I relate that simple story to say this: Marriage relationships are like bridges. They carry a lot of weight, are weakened by stress, and break down by neglect. Too often, we treat our marriages like David treated that bridge, putting off the hard work of restoration because everything seems to be working well enough for the moment. But such neglect exponentially multiplies future problems.

The good news is that there is a way to repair the breach, rebuild the bridge, and restore relationships that are broken.

The Dumbest Time of My Life

"I want a divorce."

Yes, those words once escaped my lips. Five years and innumerable stupid decisions into my marriage, I uttered what should have never been said. I was twenty-three, angry and bitter at God for the many hurtful situations and disappointments that I felt he had caused in my life. I gave up on God and moved far away from him, resulting in serious spiritual, emotional, and relational trouble. Such colossal failures in my life couldn't help but to negatively affect my young marriage.

Thank God for his patience and my wife's endurance. We're still together because God rescued me from my idiocy and healed my relationship both with him and my wife. What He's done for me I know he can do for you. He can heal broken hearts, broken lives, and broken marriages. I know this to be true from my own life, from those I've counseled, and from what I read in the Bible.

God heals, and it's a miraculous thing to witness when a marriage shattered like broken pottery is slowly remade into something stronger and more beautiful than it ever was before.

The Starting Point for Forgiveness and Healing

Forgiveness is not always a one-time event. It is a process that people often have to work through multiple times for the same issue. Forgiveness involves both the mind and the heart. Many people fool themselves into thinking they've forgiven someone else since they've verbally said, "I forgive you." Sometimes this is done to quickly move past a troubling problem without addressing its root cause. At other times, the words are spoken in order to elicit a desired response from the one who's inflicted pain. While it is important to vocalize forgiveness, this should happen after particular changes within the heart have occurred. "What you say flows from what is in your heart" (Luke 6:45b, NLT).

I relate that warning to say this: the starting point for forgiveness begins with you and what you choose to hold on to in your heart.

If there's one central word we should focus on when it comes to forgiveness, I believe it's *surrender*. In our culture, we consider surrendering as an act of giving up or giving in. In other words, we don't value surrendering, but I think that's because we have a low view of what it really means, especially in relation to our Christian walk. To surrender to God is to embrace his path and yield to his way. Surrendering means letting go of our way as we accept and follow his plans. To surrender is to trust. Nowhere does Jesus make this more clear than in Mark 8:34b-36: "If anyone would come after me, he must deny himself and take up his cross and follow me. For whoever wants to save his life will lose it, but whoever loses his life for me and for the gospel will save it. What good is it for a man to gain the whole world, yet forfeit his soul?"

In my New Revised Bubna Translation, I'd rephrase Jesus's last question to fit this book: "What good is it for a spouse to gain the whole world, yet forfeit his or her marriage?" But I'm getting a little ahead of myself.

Surrendering is central to the Christian faith. It's what we do when we accept Christ into our lives. We surrender our lives to him, trusting him to guide us much better than we can guide ourselves.

So what does this broad concept of surrendering have to do with forgiveness in marriage? Everything. When we surrender to God's way, we'll discover and experience his power to heal, and *every* marriage can benefit from that.

A Clear but Challenging Path to Forgiveness

If your marriage is in a "good place" right now, keep reading. Because we're human, no marriage stays in that good place forever. For issues both large and small, we need to practice the art of forgiveness on a consistent basis, especially in our marriages. In other words, though this section specifically deals with forgiveness between two struggling people in a covenant marriage, I believe these biblically based ideas will provide you with keen insight into how to live a life of forgiveness that extends to all of your relationships.

1. Surrender your past mistakes and learn to forgive.

First, learn to see yourself the way God sees you. Often, seeking forgiveness from someone else means first forgiving yourself. Remind yourself of the Bible's most well-known sentence in John 3:16: "For God so loved the world." That "world" includes you. Meditate on the truth of God's great forgiveness of every single one of your shortcomings, past, present, and future.

When someone who needs to forgive someone else fully realizes how much God has forgiven them, the path to forgiveness suddenly becomes clear. Paul said it well in Colossians 3:13b: "Forgive as the Lord forgave you." Those are simple words easily affirmed in our minds, but acting upon that command is often challenging. We justify our reticence toward forgiveness by claiming we're not God, by rationalizing our bitterness, anger, or hatred as normal human emotions that anyone in our same situation would feel. But when we wrap ourselves in such isolating thoughts, we blind ourselves to the truth of God's immense forgiveness *of us*. He loved, loves, and will love us *regardless* of what we've done.

One of my favorite sections in the Bible comes from Romans 8:38-39 because it explicitly states what separates us from the love of God: "For I am convinced that neither death nor life, neither angels nor demons, neither the present nor the future, nor any powers, neither height nor depth, nor anything else in all creation, will be able to separate us from the love of God that is in Christ Jesus our Lord." *Nothing* separates us from the love of God that is in Christ Jesus. Let that fully, wholly, and deeply soak into your soul. When we begin to grasp the eternally loving and forgiving nature of God in Christ, we know that we must extend grace to *all* as all grace has been extended to *us*. You must forgive as you've been forgiven because you'll never have to forgive someone more than God's already forgiven you.

Even though we might understand this concept, it won't take root as a lifestyle until we're forced to forgive someone who's deeply hurt us. Nowhere was this more evident to me than in light of a tragic story of youthful recklessness and mature, godly forgiveness. Seventeen-year-olds Tom and Allen were best buddies, and their parents were friends with each other as well. When Tom and Allen approached a railroad crossing one day, Tom gunned his car to cross the tracks, even though they were three cars back. He never saw the train that hit them, tossing Tom from the car and instantly killing Allen.

Who would blame Allen's parents for spewing hatred at Tom and his family for Tom's foolish impatience? How could such a deep and painful rift between friends be healed? Through the hard art of forgiveness. Allen's parents knew that Tom had suffered enough in the realization that his actions had cost his close friend his life. They also knew that Allen himself would have wanted them to forgive Tom, to love him, and to move on and seek healing. So they *chose* to surrender their right to anger and bitterness. They chose to forgive.

If such an incredibly painful transgression can be forgiven, and if God has forgiven you more than you know, why can't you forgive your spouse?

2. Surrender your present realities and learn to hope.

We're a quick-fix society, so I hate to break it to you, but forgiveness is anything but a quick-fix. Like I said before, you can't simply say, "I forgive you" and honestly be done with the process of forgiveness. True forgiveness typically takes time, and it's often made more difficult when we fail to see signs of progress. What do I mean by that?

When you choose to forgive your spouse, they may still be acting like a jerk. Countless couples have told me, "I've forgiven my spouse, but I don't think they're ever going to change." I hate to break this to you as well: *you're not going to change them.* Only God can affect heart change. God can use your forgiveness as a catalyst for their change, but you can't expect immediate results, especially if the problems in your marriage run deep.

When I talk about surrendering your present realities, I'm not talking about ignoring reality. Pretending that no problems exist just makes your problems that much worse. Rather, you should learn how *not* to fixate on your present realities and focus on God. It's so easy for us to become consumed by how we've been hurt, or how we think the other person ought to respond to us, but these are cul-de-sac streets on the road to forgiveness that just make us go in circles. When we choose to focus on God and see our circumstances in light of his ways, we're surrendering our vain efforts to be our spouse's Holy Spirit. (Read that again!)

Consider the story in Matthew 14 when Jesus calls Peter out of a boat to walk on water. The second that Peter takes his focus off Christ and places it onto his present and precarious circumstances, he sinks. There's much going on in that simple and incredible story, but the essential illustration is clear: we'll sink when we take our eyes off Christ. When we choose to focus on Christ instead of our present trials, we place our hope in him, we cast our cares on him, and we concern ourselves more with allowing God to mold our character rather than us trying in vain to change our spouse's character.

Learning to place our hope in Christ, especially in regard to transforming a troublesome marriage into a God-reflecting relationship, we must develop particular attitudes about ourselves:

- I know that my spouse and I have some unresolved issues.
- I accept that healing is a process that takes times.
- This process can be a painful journey. (And I will get help when needed.)
- There are some things that still need to change.
- But I'm going to surrender to God *my* plan to *fix* my spouse.
- Because ultimately, my hope is in him! (And not in me, my spouse, or anything else the world offers as a third-rate imitation.)

When you begin to feel yourself focusing too much on your present situation, read Psalm 62:5-7: "Find rest, O my soul, in God alone; my hope comes from him. He alone is my rock and my salvation; he is my fortress, I will not be shaken. My salvation and my honor depend on God; he is my mighty rock, and my refuge" (emphasis added).

3. Surrender your future fears and learn to trust.

Growing up, I was jealous of my sister Kim. She slept upstairs while my brothers and I slept in the basement. She often got to stay up later than us. Because of the preferential treatment I saw, I decided to take my revenge in a way that only a young boy can devise. One night, I waited under her bed. Just as she was about to fall asleep, I screamed as I grabbed her. She was terrified. I was delighted. Mission accomplished. But what I thought was a one-time prank turned into a lifelong fear. She still looks under the bed to make sure no one's there.

When we're hurt, whether physically or emotionally, we fear being hurt the same way again. This is especially true in marriages, where the kinds of hurt spouses can inflict on each other open gaping wounds. When trust has been broken—or shattered as in most affairs—the victimized spouse faces a near insurmountable obstacle in learning to trust their spouse ever again. When married couples do the hard work of reconciliation, they must learn to deal with fear. Surrendering our fears is an integral part of forgiveness. Seldom do we actually want to face our fears, but it's a necessary step toward whole forgiveness.

Hurt spouses often tell me some variant of: "Trust has to be earned. I'll trust him again if he proves himself trustworthy." I agree that trust must be earned and that it takes time, but I disagree with where they should focus that trust. I don't ask that person to blindly or immediately trust in the person who hurt them.

I ask them to trust in God. Are you starting to sense a theme?

In fact, I don't believe a hurt spouse will ever learn to truly trust their husband or wife until they first and foremost learn to release their legitimate fears and trust in God. In Isaiah 26:3-4, the prophet says, "You will keep in perfect peace all who trust in you, whose thoughts are fixed on you! Trust in the Lord always, for the Lord God is the eternal Rock." In other words, the "path to perfect peace" is trusting in God.

Plus, when we trust God with our future, it eradicates a thousand "What if?" questions our insecure, untrusting minds devise in the aftermath of a serious breach of trust in our marriages. Asking these questions keeps you driving around the same cul-de-sac as focusing on the other person because it's still *focusing on the other person*. "What if he breaks my heart again? What if she leaves me? What if he goes back to his old habits? What if she never talks to me again?" When you find yourself lost in a maze of countless possibilities (which you can never know and can't control), flip the focus of the question. "What if *I* choose to forgive? What if *I* opt to stay? What if

God wants our marriage to succeed? What if *I* allow *God* to change my heart first?"

When we learn how to face our fears and surrender our future, we live out an old Christian cliché whose truth rings deep: I don't know what the future holds, but I know Who holds my future. As "the eternal Rock," we can count on his never-changing, ever-lasting nature to quiet our fears and take care of our future.

Too few understand what forgiveness means. It's not about ignoring or forgetting the wrong. It's not about excusing or justifying the evil done to us. Neither is it about pretending that all is well or denying sin's consequences.

Forgiveness is:

- Choosing to surrender our right for revenge (Rom. 12:19).
- Choosing to bless and love rather than curse and hate (Matt. 5:44; Rom. 12:14).
- Choosing to keep no record of wrong (1 Cor. 13:5).
- Choosing to be merciful and compassionate as God has been with us (Matt. 5:7; Col. 3:12-13).
- Choosing to let go and surrender the primary care of our hearts, lives, and future to the Father (Luke 23:34).
- Choosing to forgive ourselves (1 Cor. 4:3).

The consequences of unforgiveness are catastrophic. When we refuse to untie the relational knot of bitterness, we end up bound and broken. But trust and surrender lead to freedom, and God wants us to live free, forgiving others as he has forgiven us. Forgiveness is not just important—it's everything.

Right now, take your pain to Jesus and find his healing, hope, and help. He will empower you to do what he calls you to do. What bitterness or anger will you forsake for the sake of love? Always remember: life is too short to live consumed by unforgiveness—especially when it comes to your marriage.

Seek forgiveness and you *will* find healing.

9

Final Thoughts

LET'S END WHERE we started: marriage is hard. That being said, marriage is also a great gift from the Father used to mold and carve us into the men and women he wants us to become.

After nearly forty years of marriage, lots of struggles, and a few trips through the valley of the shadow of death in our relationship, I can tell you it's worth it.

Always fun? Nope.

Always easy? Absolutely not.

Always good for us? Yes.

Laura and I have learned the greatest secret of survival: *stay the course*.

- When you're not sure you even like each other, let alone love each other, *stay the course* and make the choice to love.

- When you're physically and emotionally exhausted, *stay the course* and take your next step in God's power. Remember, his grace is made perfect in your weakness.
- When the obstacle in your face overwhelms you, *stay the course* and fix your eyes on Jesus, who is the pioneer and perfecter of your faith. You are not alone.
- When you're hurting and devastated by your spouse's sin or immaturity, *stay the course* and trust that God is bigger than your spouse and more committed to their growth than you can imagine.

One last thing: for many of you, this book is a needed refresher. For others, you have learned new truths about yourself and your marriage. For some, however, it has pushed all sorts of emotional buttons, and you might be terribly discouraged at this point.

I beg you, humble yourself and get help. Find a Christian counselor or pastor who can walk you through the process of healing. Get a marriage mentor who will support you and hold you accountable.

Far too often, couples wait too long, and by the time they end up reaching out for help, their marriage is on its final count. Why do they wait? Pride. But as Solomon wrote, "Pride goes before destruction, a haughty spirit before a fall" (Proverbs 16:18).

The stakes are high. In our culture, surviving—let alone thriving—in a long-term relationship is challenging. But in Christ all things are possible, including the healing and maturity of your marriage.

So *stay the course*, and you'll never regret it. Keep going. Be a lifelong learner, commit to personal and spiritual growth, and then watch what God will do in you and your marriage.

May I pray for you?

Father, you created the institution of marriage, but sometimes we feel so weighed down by marital struggles we want to give up and run away. Sometimes, the most important person in our lives is the most hurtful. Help us to love as you love. Help us to forgive as You forgive us. Help us to believe that You can do some of Your best resurrection work despite the occasional darkness and stench of death in our marriages. Cover us with grace and empower us with hope. Make our marriages shine in a broken culture that is far from You. Amen.

Acknowledgements

If it takes a village to raise a healthy child, it takes a great editor to produce a good book. Blake Atwood is that guy, and I am so grateful for his support on this project.

Additionally, I am indebted to my daughter, Jessica Harris, for her proofing expertise, and her female insights that helped immensely.

Of course, my greatest tribute belongs to my best friend and partner in the marriage journey, my wife Laura. You, my love, have made me a better me.

Marriage Communication Inventory

To discover the health of your communication with your spouse, answer the following twelve questions with a simple YES or NO.

1. Do you have special times when you and your spouse are alone and talk?

❏ Yes ❏ No

2. Do you listen to your spouse and does he or she know that he or she has your undivided attention?

❏ Yes ❏ No

3. Do you use "emotional word pictures" to help in the communication process?

❏ Yes ❏ No

4. Are you free to discuss any subject(s) with your spouse?

❏ Yes ❏ No

5. Do you really enjoy talking with your spouse?

❏ Yes ❏ No

6. More often than not, do you look directly at your spouse when you talk?

❏ Yes ❏ No

7. Do you help your spouse feel that his or her opinions and beliefs are important and valuable?

❏ Yes ❏ No

8. Are you careful not to interrupt your spouse before he or she has finished speaking?

❏ Yes ❏ No

9. Do you show interest in the activities of your spouse? Do you ask him or her questions about what he or she is doing or what he or she likes?

❏ Yes ❏ No

10. Does your spouse feel that he or she can talk with you about anything without being judged or put down?

❏ Yes ❏ No

11. Are you careful to resolve issues between the two of you that would make communication difficult?

❏ Yes ❏ No

12. Would you rather talk with your spouse about a matter before you speak with anyone else?

❏ Yes ❏ No

Answer Key

10-12 yes answers = Your communication skills are great!

7-9 yes answers = Your communication skills need some honing.

0-6 yes answers = Your communication skills need a major overhaul!

Check my recommended reads for more on developing healthy communication skills in your marriage.

Affection Reflection

1. On a scale of one to ten, with ten being "very affectionate," how affectionate am I toward my spouse? How would he or she rate me?

2. Is affection the "environment" for our marriage? If not, how can I contribute to developing this environment in our relationship?

3. In what specific ways do I show my spouse affection? What are some affectionate "acts" I think he or she would probably enjoy?

4. What are some ways in which I would like to receive affection?

5. Would I find it easier to make love if I felt my spouse were truly interested in me and affectionate toward me?

6. Would I be willing to have my spouse "coach" me in how to show more affection in the ways he or she really likes?

Sex Opinion Questionnaire and Couples Discussion Guideline

The primary intent of this exercise is to encourage couples to learn to communicate with each other regarding their beliefs, desires (likes and dislikes), expectations, and feelings about sex. Remember to "speak the truth in love." Be kind, wise, and sensitive to your spouse.

Circle the number(s) which best describes how you feel. Do this independently, then set a time to discuss your answers with your spouse.

1. As an aspect of building and maintaining a relationship, sex is:

1.   Extremely important
2.   Important
3.   Relatively unimportant
4.   Unimportant
5.   Counterproductive

2. My parent's influence on me in the area of sexuality was:

1. They didn't talk about sex.
2. They taught me "the facts," but not the joy of sex.
3. They adequately prepared me for my spouse.

3. I would like sexual intercourse:

1. More often
2. Present frequency is just right
3. Less Often

4. I think my spouse would like sexual intercourse:

1. More often
2. Present frequency is just right
3. Less Often

5. All things considered, my sex life is:

1. Perfect
2. Satisfactory
3. Not quite satisfactory
4. Less than satisfactory
5. Desperate

6. All things considered, I think my spouse thinks our sex life is:

1. Perfect
2. Satisfactory
3. Not quite satisfactory
4. Less than satisfactory
5. Desperate

7. My spouse and I talk about sex:

1. Too much
2. Often and freely
3. Not enough
4. Rarely

8. Which statement(s) is most accurate:

1. We don't talk much during love-making.
2. I find it difficult to tell my spouse what I like or dislike about love-making.
3. My spouse rarely tells me what he or she likes or dislikes in love-making.

9. By the way my spouse reacts to me, I'd say he or she finds me:

1. Very attractive sexually
2. Attractive sexually
3. Sometimes attractive sexually
4. Sexually unattractive

10. I prefer sexual intercourse:

1. In bed, under the covers, with the lights off.
2. On the bed with some lights on.
3. On the floor, lights on or off.
4. Anywhere in the house our imagination takes us.

11. I would prefer my spouse to be:

1. More dominant and aggressive sexually
2. Less dominant and aggressive sexually
3. As they are now

12. The part of lovemaking I usually wish would last longer is:

1. Foreplay (Arousal)
2. Pre-climax (Plateau)

3.   Climax

4.   Post-climax loving (Resolution)

13. Oral sex is:

1.   Repulsive

2.   An uncomfortable idea

3.   An interesting idea that I would be willing to learn more about

4.   Occasionally acceptable

5.   A delightful practice

14. Regarding sexual desire I am:

1.   Resistant

2.   Slow

3.   Sporadic

4.   Consistent

5.   Eager

15. Our sex life is:

1.   Subdued (i.e. pretty unexciting and somewhat hindered)

2.   Predictable (i.e. kinda boring most of the time)

3.   Lively and Creative

16. Regarding further "sexual education" I am:

1. Not willing to grow or learn anything more
2. Willing to learn, but bashful and a little afraid
3. Willing to learn and excited about the possibilities of continued growth in this area
4. Take me to a bookstore now

17. During foreplay (i.e. the arousal stage) I like/would like my spouse to:

18. I believe birth control is the responsibility of a husband / wife / couple (circle one) because:

19. The question about sex that I've always wanted to ask (but didn't know how) is:

Recommended Reading

Communication

- *The Language of Love*, Gary Smalley & John Trent
- *7 Things He'll Never Tell You*, Dr. Kevin Leman
- *Communication, Sex & Money*, Edwin Louis Cole
- *The Five Love Languages*, Gary Chapman

Male and Female Differences

- *Men & Women: Enjoying the Difference*, Dr. Larry Crabb
- *Men Are Clams, Women Are Crowbars*, David Clarke, Ph.D.
- *If Only He Knew*, Gary Smalley
- *5 Love Needs of Men & Women*, Dr. Gary & Barbara Rosberg
- *His Needs, Her Needs*, Willard F. Harley, Jr.

Affairs

- *The Myth of the Greener Grass*, J. Allan Petersen
- *Loving Your Marriage Enough to Protect It*, Jerry B. Jenkins

Sex

- *60 Things God Said About Sex*, Lester Sumrall
- *Sexual Intimacy in Marriage*, William Cutrer, MD & Sandra Glahn
- *Intimate Issues*, Linda Dillow & Lorraine Pintus
- *A Celebration of Sex*, Dr. Douglas E. Rosenau
- *The Gift of Sex*, Clifford and Joyce Penner
- *Intended for Pleasure*, Ed Wheat, M.D. & Gaye Wheat

Marriage in General

- *Risking Intimacy*, Nancy Groom
- *Fit to Be Tied*, Bill & Lynne Hybels
- *Lonely Husbands, Lonely Wives*, Dennis Rainey
- *Love & Respect*, Dr. Emerson Eggerichs
- *When Two Become One*, Christopher & Rachel McCluskey
- *The Joy of Committed Love*, Gary Smalley
- *Making Love Last Forever*, Gary Smalley
- *Love is a Decision*, Gary Smalley

About the Authors

Kurt W. Bubna published his first book, _Epic Grace ~ Chronicles of a Recovering Idiot_, with Tyndale in 2013. He is an active blogger (kurtbubna.com), and the Sr. Pastor of Eastpoint Church in Spokane Valley, Washington. He and his wife, Laura, have been married for nearly forty years and have four grown children and four grandchildren.

Blake Atwood is a freelance writer and editor at EditFor.me who helps pastors turn their weekend messages into long-lasting, life-enhancing books. He is also the author of _The Gospel According to Breaking Bad_.

Quality Editing and Writing Services

"As a published author, blogger, and pastor, I have worked with several editors. In my experience, Blake Atwood is one of the best. He's professional, timely, easy to work with, and he has an uncanny ability to get in your head and write with your voice. Atwood has my highest recommendation." — Kurt W. Bubna, author of *Epic Grace*

"Blake's editing, writing, organization, and efficiency are outstanding. He made my manuscript *much* better and I highly recommend his services." — Mark Riggins, author of *STUCK: When You Want to Forgive But Don't Know How*

Get a quote within 48 hours at www.editfor.me.

Notes, Quotes, & Things I Want to Remember

18729021R00099

Made in the USA
San Bernardino, CA
26 January 2015